"**What is a just, a Jewish way,** to peace? How can Israel restore herself to economic, social and political health, and how can the Diaspora best be of assistance in this major effort? How can Israel build the values and ideals of Judaism into her way of life? What is the proper relationship between Israel and the Diaspora?"

"**It may be that Jewish influence** in America has already achieved and passed its peak, and that future years may witness its relative decline, due chiefly to the upward thrust and increasing relative influence of the much larger, rapidly growing and ever more assertive claims of the Black, Puerto Rican and Mexican-American communities..."

"**In the past three decades,** Israel has served most Western Jews as a surrogate for the traditional Judaism from which they have strayed. Concern and support for Israel increasingly became the chief source and expression of their sense of Jewish identity....A relatively secure Israel...could scarcely be expected to evoke the same kind of intensity of response and commitment.... Most Diaspora Jews would increasingly need to find new stimuli to maintain their sense of Jewish identity, or that sense would tend to weaken."

"**Many, perhaps most, Israelis** seem to hold quite parochial views about the Diaspora.... The classic Zionist ideology which denigrates the prospects for a secure or meaningful Jewish existence in the Diaspora, and which conceives of Diaspora existence as living in exile, is remote from the thinking of most Jews who live in free democratic societies, and is not conducive to effective communications between Israelis and emancipated and secular Diaspora Jews."

# FROM *"ISSUES FACING WORLD JEWRY"*

**"Increasing difficulties** [are] posed for Jewish leaders when they are expected unquestioningly to support Israel's policies regardless of the private reservations they may have about them."

**"Unless somehow checked,** a prolonged and deep decline in Jewish population throughout the Diaspora will occur in the decades ahead."

**"The failure to seek or achieve** the active involvement of more than a small minority of outstanding Jewish intellectuals in Jewish communal life has constituted a serious weakness."

**"Generational change...** combined with occupational shifts from business to the professions and academia...presage a decline in communal fund-raising."

**"Should American Jewry continue to extend** financial and other assistance to Soviet Jews who prefer to immigrate to the United States, or should the American Jewish community, by withholding such assistance, increase the relative attractions of Israel and thus help to lower the 'dropout' rate among Jews leaving the Soviet Union?"

**"A plethora of American Jewish organizations...** are engaged in overlapping or duplicate activities which result in work lacking in depth and waste of available resources."

**"The better off the Jews are** as individuals, the less they tend to be concerned with their Jewishness."

# FROM *"ISSUES FACING WORLD JEWRY"*

**"Israel's remarkable achievements** in industry, agriculture and other productive sectors, in science, education and technology, in social fields, and in institutional development...has come at a price. It has brought with it a certain materialism and a growing number of personal discontents. These stand out more glaringly in the case of Israel because they contrast sharply with the idealism and egalitarianism of the early Zionists."

**"There is a general sense** that the Jewish goals and values Zionists hoped would flourish in a Jewish state are in an advanced state of erosion and are in danger of being permanently lost.... Israel today—quite apart from the vital problems of peace and security — is a troubled, anxious and demoralized society."

**"The religious monopoly** exercised by the Orthodox rabbinate in Israel with the official sanction of the government [is] offensive to Conservative and Reform Jewry, as well as to many secular Jews, in the Diaspora."

**"Israel denigrates** [the problem of its own emigrants] and is embarrassed by the undiagnosed phenomenon they represent... If so many of its own people have elected to leave Israel, should not Israel be asking itself some rather basic questions?"

**"Independent Diaspora judgments** require full expression in an uninhibited dialogue of the grave doubts and concerns occasioned by Israel's positions and policies."

# ISSUES FACING WORLD JEWRY

A Report of the International
Economic and Social Commission
of the World Jewish Congress

# ISSUES FACING WORLD JEWRY

Originally published under the title
*THE IMPLICATIONS OF ISRAEL-ARAB PEACE
FOR WORLD JEWRY*

Prepared for the Commission by
Louis J. Walinsky
with the collaboration of Prof. Se'ev Hirsch

**Commentary by
Abba Eban**

HERSHEL SHANKS, PUBLISHER, WASHINGTON, D.C.

# Members of The Commission

**DR. ISAIAH FRANK** *(UNITED STATES)*.
Economist and educator. Various positions in State Department, including director, Office of International Trade, director, Office of International Financial and Developmental Affairs, Deputy Assistant Secretary for Economic Affairs; professor, International Economics, Johns Hopkins University; Author: *The European Common Market: An Analysis of Commercial Policy.*

**DR. MOSHE BENNO GITTER** *(ISRAEL)*.
Vice-Chairman, I.D.B. Bankholding Corp.; Vice-Chairman, Israel Industrial Development Bank and Discount Bank Investment Corp.; director, Israel Discount Bank, Barclays Discount Bank, and Israel Corp.

**JEROLD C. HOFFBERGER** *(UNITED STATES)*.
Chairman, Executive Committee, Fairchild Industries; Chairman, United Israel Appeal; Chairman, S.T.L., Inc., Diversified Resource Management Ltd.; President, Baltimore Baseball Club, Inc.; director, Hoffberger Foundation Inc.; Maryland National Bank; director, American Joint Distribution Committee; Honorary Director and past President, Council of Jewish Federations.

**ERNEST I. JAPHET** *(ISRAEL)*.
Banker. Managing director, chief executive officer, chairman of the board, Union Bank of Israel, Ltd., Bank Leumi Investment Co. Ltd.; Deputy Chairman, Board of Governors Hebrew University; Board of Governors, Tel-Aviv University, Technion, Haifa University, Ben-Gurion University.

**BURTON JOSEPH** *(UNITED STATES)*.
President, I. S. Joseph Co.; Minneapolis Human Relations Commission, former treasurer and national chairman, National Commission of the Anti-Defamation League of B'nai B'rith; trustee, Board of Governors, Hebrew Union College — Jewish Institute of Religion.

**SOL KANEE, O.C.** *(CANADA)*.
Treasurer, World Jewish Congress; director, Bank of Canada; chairman, Soo Line Mills Ltd.; director, Bank of Canada, Executive Committee; former chairman, Federal Business Development Bank; former chairman, Royal Winnipeg Ballet, United Way of Greater Winnipeg.

**MAX KARL** *(UNITED STATES)*.
Founder and chairman, Mortgage Guaranty Insurance Co. Milwaukee; President, Mortgage Insurance Companies of America; director, First Wisconsin National Bank and Affiliates; member, Advisory Committee on Federal Home Loan Mortgage Corp.; chairman, Governor's Council on Economic Development; director, United Jewish Appeal, United Israel Appeal, United HIAS Service, Council of Jewish Federations.

**DR. HENRY KAUFMAN** *(UNITED STATES)*.
Investment analyst. General partner and member of executive committee, Salomon Brothers; chairman of research, Salomon Brothers; former economist, Federal Reserve Bank of New York; Board of Governors, Tel-Aviv University.

**ISRAEL KLABIN** *(BRAZIL)*.
Former Mayor, Rio de Janeiro. Managing partner, Klabin Irmãos and Cia.

**LORD HAROLD LEVER** *(ENGLAND)*.
Member of Parliament for 34 years; former Financial Secretary to the Treasury, Paymaster General, Chairman of the Public Accounts Committee. Cabinet member and financial adviser to the Prime Minister.

**JACOB LEVINSON** *(ISRAEL)*.
Chairman, Board of Directors, Bank Hapoalim B.M. and Ampal American Israel Corp.

**MORRIS LEVINSON** *(UNITED STATES)*.
President, Associated Products, Inc., President, Center for the Study of Democratic Institutions.

# Table of Contents

# Publisher's Forward

I decided to reprint this report simply because, in my judgment, it was the most important Jewish document I had read in years. After I had made my decision and the World Jewish Congress agreed, I learned that I was not alone in my assessment:

The *Jerusalem Post* in an editorial had called it a "historic" document. A staff writer of the paper called it "essentially true and monumentally important" in his analysis. Chaim Bermant in the *London Jewish Chronicle* called it "a work of historic importance." According to Richard Yaffe in *Israel Horizons*, it was "one of the outstanding Jewish documents of recent years.... A taking-off point for a worldwide discussion of where we are heading, and where we want to go."

Despite what the Jewish Telegraphic Agency referred to as the "furor" created in Jerusalem when the report was released in early 1981, when I sought to discuss the report with my friends — many of whom consider themselves Jewish communal leaders — almost none of them knew of the report, let alone had read it. A few said, yes, they thought (but were not sure) they had heard of it, perhaps had seen some reference to it in *Moment* or the *Jerusalem Post*, but that was all. Although it may have been a work of historic importance, hardly anyone seemed to know about it — a boulder that had fallen into the lake without creating a ripple — at least at the local level.

In my judgment, this report should be studied and discussed by every person who considers himself or herself a concerned Jew or a Jewish community leader. Therefore, despite the fact that several Jewish publishers turned down the project as commercially unfeasible, I was confirmed in my decision to reprint the report and thus to make it available far more widely than the original edition.

Where the report has been discussed, it is considered not only important, but highly controversial—and this may be part of the reason why it has not found its way down to the local community leadership. The World Zionist Executive, meeting in plenary session, adopted a formal statement on the report saying its "importance was exaggerated" and expressing confidence that "the World Jewish Congress will not endorse this paper." The statement of the World Zionist Executive criticized the report for being "flippant" and "rashly made," of "having been written without consulting those involved in the areas discussed." The *Jerusalem Post* predicted that the report "will probably be rejected by the vast majority of Israelis, right and left. What is far less certain is that it will similarly be spurned by the majority of Jews calling themselves Zionists in the Diaspora." Abba Eban conceded the report's "healthy realism," but found its tone "tutellary [and] patronizing." In some ways, it was "dangerous," he said.

Few will agree with everything in the report. I certainly don't. But I do believe that the issues which the report raises should be discussed, and widely discussed, at the local community level. The more influential the views of local community leaders become, the more democratic, the more participatory and the healthier the Jewish community will be.

The reprinting of this report implies agreement with only one of its conclusions — that the issues facing world Jewry, including the most sensitive disagreements, should be openly, widely, freely and publicly discussed. We should not suppress our doubts and concerns for fear of exposing internal disagreement within the Jewish community. The risk is far greater that we shall lose the benefit of our collective wisdom than that our enemies will find aid and comfort in our disagreements. This essentially is nothing more than the age-old Jewish commitment to free speech.

The importance of this report therefore lies in the frank, searching and provocative manner in which divisive and sensitive issues are explored — the failure of Diaspora Jews to emigrate to Israel, the permanence of a healthy Diaspora despite classic Zionist doctrine, the divisions and disappointments in Israeli society, the nature of Israel-Diaspora relations, the extent to which Diaspora Jews should involve themselves in Israel's policies and problems, the religious monopoly exercised by the Orthodox rabbinate in Israel with the official sanction of the government, the Jewish demographic crisis, the failure of the Jewish community to involve outstanding Jewish intellectuals in its work, the wasteful and duplicative activities of the plethora of American Jewish organizations, the fading of Jewish influence in America, the coming crisis in Jewish fundraising, and on and on.

This report was originally published under the title "The Implications of Israel-Arab Peace for World Jewry." Unhappily, true Israel-Arab peace seems so remote at the moment that if this were the major premise of the report, it would be largely irrelevant. In fact, as the report itself recognizes, "What we have produced is perhaps not so much a study of the implications and consequences of peace as it is a study of the tension-packed, issue-torn and problematic outlook for world Jewry in the 1980's." Thus the issues which the report addresses are fundamental and far-reaching regardless of prospects for Israel-Arab peace. As Yosef Goell noted in the *Jerusalem Post*, "this report is a *tour d'horizon* of the state of affairs in the Jewish world." Accordingly, the title I have adopted is not only far less unwieldly than the original, but it is also more accurate. As so frequently happens, so with the original title of the report: Events overtake us.

In the flush of hope following President Sadat's 1977 journey to Jerusalem and the Camp David accords that followed, peace seemed a realistic prospect. Philip Klutznick, the president of the World Jewish Congress (he resigned to accept President Carter's appointment as Secretary of Commerce), wisely appointed an *ad hoc* commission of the World Jewish Congress to consider the implications for broader Jewish issues of the peace which seemed within grasp.

A truly blue-ribbon commission composed of an international group of leading academics, political leaders, communal leaders, businessmen and labor leaders from Israel and the Diaspora worked for two years to produce its report. It soon became clear to them that to be meaningful, the report would have to address not the ephemeral, but the broader issues, issues that must be faced regardless of the peregrinations of the peace process. Thus the report is not tied to the success or failure of Israel's continuing efforts to secure a just and lasting peace. It is truly a discussion of "Issues Facing World Jewry."

It is the publisher's hope that this report will be read, studied, analyzed and discussed, and that out of this process the Jewish community of the world will come a bit closer to facing and resolving these difficult issues. Our survival depends on it.

Hershel Shanks

September, 1981
Washington, D.C.

# Preface

President Sadat's historic reception in Jerusalem in November 1977 signified, for the first time in the thirty-year life of the State of Israel, that peace between Israel and the Arab states was a distinct possibility. That is why, on the wise initiative of its then President Philip M. Klutznick (who took leave thereafter to serve as U.S. Secretary of Commerce), the World Jewish Congress created the International Economic and Social Commission to study and report on the implications of peace for world Jewry. We were delighted that so many outstanding Jews, distinguished for their accomplishments in Jewish communal affairs, business and industry, economics, finance and the academic world, from North and South America, Europe and Israel, consented to participate, and that Baron Guy de Rothschild undertook to serve as Chairman of the Commission.

After nearly two years of intensive study, the Commission has now presented its report. Its independent conclusions and recommendations are naturally those of the Commission alone — the World Jewish Congress is neither responsible for nor committed to accept or support any of them. We do believe however that this thoughtful, sensitive and significant report warrants the serious consideration of concerned Jews everywhere. We shall submit this report for consideration at the Plenary Assembly of the World Jewish Congress, to be held in Jerusalem January 18-23, 1981, and make it available for a wider distribution as well.

To Chairman Guy de Rothschild and all the members of the Commission, we extend our sincere thanks for the service they have rendered to the Jewish people.

Edgar M. Bronfman
Acting President
World Jewish Congress

December 1980

# Letter of Transmittal

To The President, World Jewish Congress:

I have the honor to transmit the final report of our Commission - "The Implications of Israel-Arab Peace for World Jewry".

This ad hoc, autonomous Commission was created by the World Jewish Congress two years ago, on the initiative of President Philip M. Klutznick (now on leave), to study and report on the implications of peace in the Middle East for Israel, the Diaspora and for Israel-Diaspora relations. We understood it to be the desire of the World Jewish Congress to stimulate and help Jewish communities everywhere to anticipate and prepare to cope with the responsibilities they may be required to face in the peace-building period. In striving to fulfill this task, which we have approached in all humility, we have sought not only to anticipate the shape of coming events, but also, to the extent we could to influence them. We hope our report will contibute to these objectives.

We decided at the outset that the purposes of our study would best be served if we aimed at the utmost we could achieve in objectivity, realism and candor. The importance of the issues with which we were concerned clearly transcended any injured feelings which might result. We have tried, equally, to be judicious and constructive in our self-criticism. The outstanding experience, talent, wisdom, dedication and expertise in planning of our members, chosen with great sagacity by Mr. Kluznick, have contributed enormously to these efforts and their results.

The report reflects a consensus, rather than a unanimity of view, among our members. It should be understood that their approval is a general one. Individual members may not agree with or find adequate all the opinions and recommendations expressed, or their precise formulation. A few have therefore filed supplementary statements. These in a sense confirm the weight we have given in our report to the problems in the Israel-Diaspora relationship, and the need for a more candid and effective dialogue to address and resolve them.

We are pleased that the World Jewish Congress will present our report to its forthcoming Plenary Assembly in Jerusalem, and that it will also be made available for a wider public distribution. Readers should of course understand that our members represent and speak for no one but themselves. The World Jewish Congress has in no way sought to guide or influence our study or its findings, and is naturally not responsible for or committed to accept any of our conclusions or recommendations.

Our report speaks for itself, and there are only two points I should make here about it. First, it has not been possible to take fully into account such recent developments as the eruption of the East Jerusalem and Golan issues and the Iraq-Iran war. Second, I am aware that, because we have concentrated our attention on the problems and concerns of world Jewry, some readers may find our report depressing or gloomy. This would be regrettable. We Jews have no way to a secure and better future unless we recognize, address and attempt to resolve the extremely serious problems we face. In calling for such recognition and action, we believe we are being constructive and basically hopeful. We *can* resolve the problems that confront us, if we see them clearly and address them with spirit, courage and determination.

I wish to convey to the members of this Commission my sincere thanks for their dedicated cooperation and invaluable contibutions to our work. Sincere thanks are due also to our many invited speakers for their outstanding presentations and the authors of the illuminating papers we studied. To Mr. Walinsky, who organized and conducted our study, and drafted the Commission's report, and to Prof. Hirsch, his associate, we owe special thanks and heartiest congratulations. Finally, on behalf of myself and all my Commission colleagues and staff, I wish to thank the World Jewish Congress and Philip M. Klutznick for affording us this opportunity to serve the Jewish people.

Sincerely,
Guy de Rothschild
Chairman

December 1980

*Part One*

# INTRODUCTION AND PERSPECTIVE

## Chapter One

# Introduction

This Commission — an *ad hoc*, autonomous body of Jewish community leaders, business men, economists, academicians, financiers and industrialists from many countries — was created by the World Jewish Congress in November, 1978 to enquire into the implications of partial or comprehensive Israel-Arab peace for Israel, for the other Jewish communities throughout the world (the Diaspora or Dispersion), and for Israel-Diaspora relations. The Commission undertook this task with a keen awareness of its potential importance for world Jewry, of the great challenges it presented, and of the many difficulties, complexities and uncertainties inescapably involved in discharging the grave responsibilities it was accepting.

From the time the full Commission first convened in March, 1979 it was clear that while the treaty then about to be signed between Israel and Egypt represented an essential and major first step on the road to Israel-Arab peace, that road would in all likelihood be a long, arduous and unpredictable one. Consideration of the implications of near and medium term partial peace with Egypt, while difficult, would be practicable. Consideration of a more general or comprehensive peace between Israel and her remaining Arab adversaries would necessarily raise a host of questions as to whether and when such a peace might be achieved and, if so, with whom and on what conditions. To deal with these many variables, it would be necessary to portray a number of alternative scenarios, all of them highly speculative. The results of such an effort could only be confusing. We decided therefore at the outset to concentrate our forward-looking effort on the implications of the Israel-Egypt peace over the near and medium term, and to deal much more briefly and only in the broadest of terms with the implications of a more general peace.

As our work proceeded, unforeseeable developments introduced new perspectives and further complicated our task. The overturn of the Shah in Iran, the advent there of a highly unstable, fundamentalist Muslim regime openly hostile to Israel and the United States, and the hostage crisis which followed soon after, constituted one such set of developments. The Soviet incursion into Afghanistan, with its manifold and dangerous implications and tensions, was another. A third was the prolonged stalemate in the West Bank (Judea and Samaria) and Gaza autonomy negotiations so essential to continuation of the peace-building process. The fourth and perhaps the most serious of these, was the outbreak of war between Iraq and Iran, which came when the drafting of this report had been completed and was in its final circulation. We had already made clear our conviction that Israel-Arab peace not equate with peace in the Middle East, and would not suffice to ensure it. The Iraq-Iran war changed this distinction from a thesis to a demonstrated fact. This to be sure serves to dramatize and strengthen the broader analysis and perspectives we have presented; but it has implications we have not been able fully to take into account. U.S. and West European policies in the Middle East have assumed that resolution of the Palestinian question would lead not only to Israel-Arab peace but also to Middle East peace and stability, and ensure the uninterrupted flow of vitally essential oil supplies. Politices based on this obviously invalidated assumption will have to be re-shaped to accommodate to a more realistic perception of existing realities. The implications of these policy shifts, and of the chain of events which may arise out of them, lie beyond the scope of our analysis.

The Palestinians and Jordan declined from the first to participate in the autonomy negotiations. Virtually all the Arab states expressed opposition to them and to the Camp David approach to peace on which they were based. After prolonged initial discussions concerned primarily with procedural matters, basic differences in the Israeli and Egyptian approaches to the autonomy emerged and became major points of contention and stumbling blocks. Under the Camp David accords, the final decision on the future of the West Bank, and resolution of the Palestinian question, were to be deferred until five years after the interim autonomy agreement. But both Israel and Egypt sought an autonomy agreement the conditions of which would ensure that the final decision five years later would not run counter to their desires. Egypt, taking a hard line, espoused an autonomy agreement which threatened almost inevitably to result in the establishment of an independent, P.L.O. led, Palestinian state. The core of her position was that the self-governing body to be created for the Autonomy should be one with full legislative powers and a voice in security arrangements. Israel, determined to prevent the evolution of an independent Palestinian state as an unacceptable threat to her security, insisted that the Autonomy's self-governing body be limited to administrative powers only, and that the right to make decisions affecting Israel's security would not be shared. Israel's controversial and much publicized settlements policies were relevant to this core issue because, as implemented by the Begin government, they suggested that Israel intended to extend indefinitely her rule or to establish sovereignty over the entire West Bank (Judea and Samaria).

In this situation, real progress on the autonomy agreement was impossible. Meanwhile, keen resentment and political agitation among West Bank Arabs found vent in violent demonstrations. These evoked counter-measures by Israeli settlers and stern control actions by the military authorities, kindling still further Arab reactions and international concerns. West European governments, in a new diplomatic initiative, not only supported Palestinian demands for self-determination, but also affirmed that the P.L.O. should be associated with the negotiations — a move which threatened to subvert the Camp David Accords and the peace effort based on them. These developments further clouded the prospects for peace, and inevitably affected the orientation of our study. Although we have tried to adhere to our original task, what we have produced is perhaps not so much a study of the implications and consequences of peace as it is a study of the tension-packed, issue-torn and problematic outlook for world Jewry in the 1980's. Our primary aim has been to identify and assess the large policy issues with which world Jewry must now be concerned and endeavor, to the extent we can, to help shape their outcomes in a constructive way.

In doing so, we have had to resolve for ourselves a problem which has been present throughout the Israel-Diaspora relationship, and which has, in recent years, become increasingly acute. Simply stated, the problem is whether Diaspora Jews should speak out publicly in criticism of perceived weaknessess in Israel's economy, social life or polity, or in the relations between Israel and the Diaspora, or even in its peace-making policies, or whether they should refrain from such candor because it may be exploited by those unfriendly or hostile to Israel and the Jewish people. In the past, this problem has generally been resolved by silence or reticent understatement. Indeed, even private dialogues between Israelis and Diaspora Jews seem often to have taken the same path. Our own resolution of this problem has been to deal candidly with serious matters which, in our opinion, have too often been swept under the rug. Anything less than frank statement at this time, we believe, would detract from the credibility and value of our report, both in the Jewish world and in the larger world around us. We also question whether such reticence in the past has indeed served Israel's best interests. The suppression of self-criticism would not disarm or silence our enemies in the future any more than it has in the past; they would merely find or invent other weapons with which to attack us. We believe rather than the security and welfare of Jews in

Israel and the Diaspora demand the open and honest expression of our beliefs and judgments. We trust that the outspoken views, analyses and recommendations presented in this report will be received in that spirit.

We note especially, in this connection, that some of the most candid and penetrating criticism that has been expressed in the areas of our concerns has come from Israeli scholars and thinkers. Opinion on these matters, obviously, is divided within both Israel and the Diaspora. The differences in view with which we are chiefly concerned, therefore, including those which involve the Israel-Diaspora relationship, are not essentially differences between Israeli Jews and Diaspora Jews, but are rather differences which exist *within* Jewish communities everywhere, including Israel. They exist, indeed, as unresolved problems within individual Jews, as well as between one Jew and another. We find these considerations additionally encouraging in the choice we have made to address them.

One theme that runs throughout our Report is the need for Israel progressively to embody in her polity and way of life the values that Judaism contributed to the world. We have emphasized the importance of this especially for the maintenance of close ties between Israel and the Diaspora. "In Israel", the rabbi says, "converge all my people's hope and national aspirations accumulated over the millenia, and from Israel I seek fulfillment of our national destiny as a light unto the nations." Our repeated emphasis on this point does not mean we consider that hard-pressed Israel *owes* it to the Diaspora somehow to be better, more pure, more noble than any other country. We mean, rather, in the sense of Ahad Ha'am, that this is what the Diaspora desperately *needs* from Israel, to sustain its sense of Jewish identity, peoplehood and attachment to Israel.

We have also had to resolve another problem — this time, one of perspective. We have been sensitive, throughout our deliberations, to the relevance and importance to our study of major trends, issues and conflicts in the wider world within which the possibilities and implications of peace for world Jewry will unfold. Developments in the Middle East will of necessity be affected in significant degree by these broader world developments, as they of course will in turn be influenced by developments in the Middle East. We believe this broader picture is of such great importance that we have decided to begin our report with a review of this worldwide perspective. Next, because the possible consequences of peace can realistically be considered only as they impinge on the current and ongoing state of affairs in Israel and the Diaspora, we shall examine at some length the more significant aspects and trends of the current world Jewish scene, as these may influence and in turn be affected by the peace-building process. We shall then, finally, be in a position to attempt to address the implications of peace and the outlook for world Jewry in the years ahead.

Before embarking on our report, it may be useful to Jewish, as well as non-Jewish, readers if we present a few key data on the world's Jewish population and its distribution.

The world's 13.7 million or so Jews* are spread among more than 100 countries on all the continents. Organized Jewish communities exist in over 80 countries. Some 3.1 million Jews, less than one-quarter of the total, live in Israel. About 10.6 million Jews, slightly more than three-quarters of the total, live in the Diaspora.

The United States, with about 5.7 million Jews, has by far the largest Jewish population, slightly more than two-fifths of the total. Figures on the Jewish population of the Soviet Union, the next largest after that of Israel, are much disputed, with estimates ranging from less than two million to some 2.7 million. The estimate used here is 2.3–2.4 million, somewhat more than one-sixth of the total. The United States, Israel and the Soviet Union combined thus account for some 11.2 million Jews, or more than four-fifths of the world's Jewish population.

The next largest Jewish communities in the world are those of, France (about 600,000), Great Britain (about 400,000), Canada and Argentina (about 300,000 each), Brazil (about 130,000) and South Africa (about 120,000). Combined, these come to close to another 2 million Jews, or nearly 14 percent of the total. Together with the United States, Israel and the Soviet Union, these nine countries accout for about 95 percent of all world Jewry. They do not embrace, however, all the communities of keen concern to world Jewry.

At its current level of close to 14 million, the world's Jewish population has partially recovered from the effects of the Holocaust, which reduced it from an estimated 16.7 million in 1939 to some 11 million by 1945. This recovery trend however does not appear likely to continue for very long. The most authoritative demographic studies currently available clearly suggest that, unless somehow checked, a prolonged and deep decline in Jewish population throughout the Diaspora will occur in the decades ahead. These projections extend, of course, far beyond the time frame of this study. But their serious policy implications provide another sobering background perspective for our study.

---

*The best recent estimates, none of them exact, range from 13.2 million to 14.3 million, with the largest discrepancy in estimates for the Soviet Union, where census figures probably understate the actuality. We are using crude mid-point figures here.

It will be obvious that in reviewing the present state of world Jewry within limited space, we shall not be able to deal separately with more than a few Jewish communities. We shall have to concentrate heavily on the very largest of them. In the case even of these, our treatment cannot attempt to be comprehensive, but must be limited to those aspects relevant to our primary purpose. Many large and important communities will of necessity be dealt with only within a larger grouping sharing many common characteristics — e.g., the emancipated Jewish communities in democratic societies. Logically, this survey would proceed from Israel to the major groupings within the Diaspora, and then to the critical question of Israel-Diaspora relations. Our study however has brought home to us with overwhelming force the fact that the Israel relation is the dominant Jewish element in the lives of most Diaspora Jews. Any enforced separation in the treatment of Diaspora communities and their relations with Israel would be artificial and weak. We have therefore dealt with Diaspora and Israel-Diaspora relations together.

*Chapter Two*

# The World Perspective

The difficulties faced by Israel, Egypt and the United States in seeking to build a wider Israel-Arab peace do not arise solely out of disparate views concerning the realization of the West Bank and Gaza autonomy called for by the Camp David accords and, five years later, the more definitive resolution of the Palestinian question. They arise also out of the hostility of the Arab (and much of the Moslem) world to the Israel-Egypt peace; out of the refusal of the P.L.O. and hard-line rejectionists like Libya, Syria and Iraq to consider peace with Israel on any terms; out of the fears of relatively "stable," pro-Western" and "moderate" Arab regimes like those in Saudi Arabia, Kuwait and the United Arab Emirates lest they be overturned by the tides of radicalism engulfing their region; out of the dominant role played within OPEC by the Arab oil-producing states, and the threat this poses to the oil lifeline of the industrial countries; out of the new and dangerous instabilities introduced into an already highly unstable Middle East by the revolution in Iran, the Soviet incursion into Afghanistan and the Iraq-Iran War; out of the growing support in Western Europe for the P.L.O. and the creation of a Palestinian state; out of Soviet opposition to the peace agreement and its machinations; out of the widespread acceptance throughout the Third World and by leftist movements of the incredible thesis that international Zionism equates with imperialism, capitalism and racism; and out of many other factors. These constitute the foreground of the broader picture with which we must be concerned.

In the two decades or so immediately following World War II, the world experienced a period of remarkable economic recovery and growth, constructive international cooperation and a progressive extension of independence and freedom throughout previously colonial Asia, the Middle East and Africa. The founding of the United Nations and its major affiliated and related agencies (IBRD, IMF, FAO, WHO, UNESCO and so on); the successful resistance to Communist expansionism in Europe and the economic recovery of war-torn Europe with

[31]

the aid of the Marshall Plan; the creation of Israel and a host of newly independent nations; the introduction of Point Four and subsequent bilateral and multilateral economic development assistance programs for the needy nations; the development of the European Economic Community; the passing of Stalin and the Soviet rift in China; the democratization, physical reconstruction and rapid economic growth of Western Germany and Japan; and general price stability and generally manageable international monetary arrangements were among the more noteworthy developments which contributed to a general aura of forward progress, confidence and betterment. The Cold War, Arab-Israel wars and the war in Korea, while seriously disturbing, dangerous and disruptive, were far outweighed by the favorable elements in the over-all picture.

Three major historical developments were chiefly responsible for radically altering this general picture, and for contributing to the increasingly dangerous state of affairs which characterizes the world today. In retrospect, the war in Vietnam was a kind of watershed which marked this turn of the tide. It not only raised serious doubts in many quarters about America's wisdom and humanity; for many, it raised serious questions about the U.S. determination to protect and maintain its world leadership position, and suggested for the first time the existence of perturbing limitations on American power. Within the United States it gave rise to a sense of frustration and guilt, serious divisiveness and a widespread belief that the exercise of American power abroad, for whatever reason, was highly immoral, as well as excessively dangerous. The youth revolt on American campuses was directed not only against the war in Vietnam, but also against received values, accepted norms and parental, institutional and governmental authority itself. Violent youth demonstrations in Europe and Japan had similar implications. Ghastly accounts of defoliation and other environmental ravages in Vietnam contributed to the rapid growth of the environmentalist movement throughout the Western world, and of a hostility to irresponsible profit-seeking without regard to air, water, soil and noise pollution. People everywhere suddenly became aware of "spaceship earth" and of environmental limitations on economic growth, as well as of prospects for natural resource depletion. Materialism, uncontrolled technology and the "Establishment" were all downgraded as a new concern for the quality of life became increasingly evident. "Liberation" movements — women's, Black's, youth's, gay's and sex — contributed to a sense that each individual was entitled "to do his own thing" with little regard for interpersonal, social or civic responsibility or discipline. Given popular mistrust, especially after Watergate, elected leaders found policy-making and governance increasingly difficult and inhibited.

At the same time, another development of grave import was unfolding. The newly independent poor nations had embarked, with high hopes and expectations, on programs of economic development. With relatively few exceptions, they found themselves disappointed and frustrated by the scanty progress most of them were able to achieve. Unable or unwilling to recognize that the responsibility for this rested largely with themselves — with the exploding population growth, distorted priorities, corruption, grandiosely unrealistic development plans, inept administration, inefficiently-managed state enterprises and counterproductive economic policies that characterized so many of them — their governments soon found it comforting to assert that their forward progress was being blocked by an unjust, exploitative, and neo-colonial international economic order. They thereupon banded together to attack the industrial nations of the "North" (excluding from this definition the Soviet Union and its allies), with demands for a "New International Economic Order." Such an order, they insisted, should provide them with assured higher prices for their raw materials, favored access to Western markets for their burgeoning manufactures, higher levels of aid, a writing down of their debts and free access to Western technology, and enable them to participate as equals in international economic decision-making, especially in those decisions required to effect international distributive "justice." These demands, generally supported by guilt-ridden liberals in Western countries and encouraged by the Soviet Union, created a new "North-South" confrontation to accompany that already existing between the Western and the communist worlds.

The Arab oil embargo late in 1973, and the opportunistic oil price quadrupling by OPEC which immediately followed, comprised the third major factor which changed the tide of postwar history. It came at a time when U.S. domestic oil production had already peaked and turned downwards, when environmentalist views and political power inhibited the vigorous exploitation of coal and nuclear energy alternatives, when a profound lack of trust in govenment resulted in the failure of appeals for voluntary conservation in energy use, and when governments throughout the Western world lacked the resolution, either to adjust effectively to the new situation imposed by OPEC, or to resist domination by the OPEC cartel with effective countermeasures within their power. The economic and political results of these failures have been catastrophic.

The enormous drain on the financial and real resources of all oil-importing countries imposed by OPEC's quantum price hikes in 1973 and since have brought prolonged economic stagnation, high rates of inflation, huge balance of payments deficits and large scale unemployment to developed and developing countries alike. Within oil-importing countries, the efforts of major economic groups to protect themselves against threatened declines in real incomes and living standards have exacerbated inflationary pressures and fragmented societies. Efforts to reduce balance of payments pressures have fostered growing demands for increasing protectionism. Economic pressures have resulted in demands for reductions in social services and inhibited defense expenditures in the face of growing Soviet military might. The international economic order has also been thrown into serious disarray. Huge and unspendable surpluses have been accumulated, chiefly by Saudi Arabia, Kuwait and the United Arab Emirates. These have been invested, mostly in liquid assets, in the Euro-banking and U.S. financial markets — the only financial markets large enough and willing to absorb them. The great international banks have in turn used such funds in large part to finance the balance of payments deficits of the non-oil producing developing countries — thus exposing themselves to the dangers of both abrupt Arab deposit withdrawals and debt repudiation or default by their hard-pressed and resentful borrowers. The United States "freeze" on Iranian assets brought home to the Arab surplus countries the possibility that a similar freeze might also, given unpredictable political developments, be imposed on their foreign assets. Lacking alternative investment outlets for their ever-growing surpluses, their obvious tendency would be to reduce production, rather than price, and keep safely in the ground the oil they do not need to sell.

The passive acceptance of OPEC's oil price, production and supply decisions by the industrial nations has conferred enormous political power on the oil producers, especially those in the Middle East. Their tremendously enhanced purchasing power, and the power of their investments, have supplemented their oil price and supply powers, and enabled them to exert significant influence over policy decision-making by oil importing governments. Third World oil importing countries, European nations and Japan have been highly vulnerable to such pressures. Even the U.S., much less dependent, relatively, on Arab oil, has also shown great deference to Saudi Arabian concerns or interests, and has from time to time bowed to them in significant ways. Europe and Japan have clearly been fearful of making decisions supportive of U.S. policies, when these have appeared to conflict even slightly with Arab views.

Concurrently, an unconscionable alliance of Third World, Communist and Arab countries virtually captured the United Nations. Third World and Communist countries have supported attacks on Israel in exchange for Arab support in attacks on the character, motives and vital interests of the "rich," "imperialist" industrial democracies. In this, the lack of reaction by non-oil producing Third World countries to their ruthless exploitation by the oil producers can only be considered very strange. Third World support of a United Nations resolution deploring the Soviet move into Afghanistan introduced the first evidence of a rift in this united front, although this rift was only a partial one.

Cynical power moves on the part of the Soviet Union in Africa, using Cuban and East German proxies in substitution for their own armed forces, and more recently by their own forces in Afghanistan, threaten to establish strategic control over the flow of oil out of the Persian Gulf to the industrial countries. Vital Western interests, and ultimately our very way of life, are thus increasingly at hazard. These Soviet threats are compounded, in the aftermath of the overturn in Iran, by the very great dangers posed by the instabilities we now discern more clearly throughout the Middle East. These arise not only out of aroused ethnic and religious group conflicts within these countries, but also out of many deep-seated envies, hatreds and conflicts among many countries in the region. These have little if anything to do with the Arab-Israel conflict. This conflict may indeed have helped considerably, over the last thirty years or so, to conceal or suppress inter-Arab and other regional animosities, for example, that between Iraq and Iran. So great is the instability of this region, and so liable is it to further outbursts even in the near future which could cut the oil lifeline and result in the economic strangulation of the Western world, that it is difficult to understand the passivity with which the West has permitted this increasingly anarchic situation to evolve in a direction which might end with the introduction of regimes committed to the decline and fall of the Western world.

In this dangerous sea of instability, independent and democratic Israel is of great positive significance to the West. The Soviet Union's recognition of this fact is shown by her antagonism to Israel and by her fostering of Arab hostility and Third World condemnation of Israel. But of the major Western powers, only the U.S. seems at all cognizant of Israel's geopolitical significance in the Middle East, and even the U.S. seems to waver between this recognition and a dangerous reliance on Saudi Arabia as a bulwark of friendly strength and stability in the region.

This dour analysis makes it quite clear that many of the most dangerous problems, tensions and conflicts presently troubling the world — the oil and energy crises, unrelenting Soviet expansionism and aggressiveness, the conflict of East-West interests and values, regional enmities, Third World frustration, envy and anti-Western feelings, resurgent and radical Islam, and Western disarray — focus on or cross paths in the Middle East. Success in building on the Israel-Egypt peace is thus of tremendous moment not only on its own account, but also because it could contribute at the same time towards easing some of these other threatening situations. *At the same time we must recognize that these broader dangers, while they are frequently confused with and may sometimes be exacerbated by the Arab-Israeli conflict, do not arise out of it, but have an independent life of their own.* Their apparent relation to it is due primarily to the fact that the countries concerned find it useful to meddle in and manipulate the Israel-Arab conflict to advance selfish and much broader national purposes of their own. This helps to explain why the Israel-Arab conflict continues to be so difficult to resolve, and suggests that its ultimate resolution may have to await the resolution of some world problems and issues which extend far beyond the Middle East and embrace other actors, more numerous and more powerful, than Israel and its immediate adversaries. The Iraq-Iran war, for example, makes it perfectly clear that resolution of the Palestinian question cannot be counted upon, as the West has supposed, to create peace and stability in the Middle East and to ensure the uninterrupted flow of vital oil supplies. The extremely dangerous situation in which the Western world now finds itself as a result of all these factors has, we suggest, a far-reaching and as yet inadequately appreciated significance for world Jewry.

Jews in the Western democracies — the U.S., Canada, Western Europe, Australia and New Zealand — have for a long time thought of themselves as emancipated and secure. Their concerns have been for Israel, for Jews in the Soviet Union and its satellites, and for Jews living under actual or potential threat in other countries. But if the position and security of the democratic countries were to become so eroded as to weaken radically their democratic way of life, then Western Jews, along with all their fellow citizens, will have suffered an enormous loss. Their dignity, self-respect and security, their full protection and equality before the law, their ability to support Israel and to help Jews in other countries — all these would be diminished or lost. What this means is that the security and well-being of Western, as well as that of all other, Jews is tied to and totally dependent on the security of the Western world. That world, we believe, is in grave danger.

This statement, in our considered judgement, is neither an exaggeration nor an over-simplication. *At the heart of the world perspective we have drawn we recognize an assault on the security, the well-being, the civilization and the values of the democratic world.* Troubled by internal doubts, fears, self-imposed inhibitions, mistrust and guilt, fearful of offending the oil and other raw materials producers, desirous of protecting and expanding established markets, and unable or unwilling to recognize, behind the spurious rhetoric of its adversaries, their malevolence and true objectives, the position of the Western world is fast eroding.

If our unhappy past, as Jews, has made us more sensitive and alert to the signs of such dangers than are most of our fellow citizens, is it not incumbent upon us, and the better part of wisdom, to try to alert them to the dangers which threaten us all? *If this be so, then the emphasis and scope of our organizational activities must be enlarged accordingly in a modified strategy designed, not only to continue our present activities, but also to sharpen Western perceptions of these broader dangers, and to strengthen Western resolve to confront and repel them.*

[36]

*Part Two*

# THE STATE
# OF
# WORLD JEWRY

# Introduction

To present in broad perspective a review of the more significant aspects and trends of the world Jewish scene, it will be useful to group the Jewish people under four major headings. We shall consider, first, the condition of the 3.1 million or so Jews living in Israel. We shall turn, next, to the 7.3 million or so Jews living emancipated lives in the free, democratic Western societies. Third, we shall review the condition of the 2.5 million or so Jews living under dictatorship in the Soviet Union and its satellites. Finally, we shall consider the nearly one million Jews who live under conditions of semi-democracy or semi-dictatorship, or which may be described variously as less than equal, or insecure, or threatening, or repressive, or disturbingly unstable, or isolated. Within this fourth group we shall consider separately the Latin-American Jewish communities and a small sampling of the others.

*Chapter Three*

# Background and Overview

Before proceeding with this review, we present here a few background comparisons and contrasts among the three largest of these groups which will help, we believe, to understand the underlying relationships among them, and help illuminate the more detailed analysis which follows. The fourth group, while smallest in numbers, is made up of many communities so diverse that they cannot usefully be discussed under a common heading.

Israeli Jews are distinguished from the other groups in many significant ways. They live in the only country where Jews constitute a large majority, and whose Jews live under Jewish sovereignty. This means that the instruments of the State can be used to advance certain Jewish communal causes which in other countries can be supported only by voluntary activities.

Nearly every Jewish child in Israel receives some Jewish education provided by the State. The Jewish citizen is compelled to make use of certain Jewish services supplied by religious institutions, such as marriage, divorce, or burial. The State can and does take measures to discourage mixed marriages, and sees to it that the Sabbath and Jewish holidays, *Kashrut*, and so on are observed by all public institutions, including the army. It subsidizes religious services and instruction. It uses diplomacy to defend and promote Jewish interests and Jewish causes abroad. It offers every Jew, under the Law of Return, the right to live in Israel.

Sovereignty thus provides the Jewish community in Israel with powerful instruments which can be used to preserve and enhance Jewish interests both inside and outside Israel. These instruments include the ability to make and enforce laws, to raise taxes and spend public money, to negotiate with foreign countries and to use force to defend vital interests.

The instruments of the State have been put at the service of Jewish causes elsewhere. Jewish emigration from communist countries and from several Arab countries was facilitated largely by Israel. In several instances, Israel was the only land to which Jewish refugees could go. In others, Israel provided the logistics and the organization which facilitated the physical movement of Jews. Diplomatic channels, in certain cases, were the only way to keep in contact with Jewish communities in distress. And diplomatic relations with friendly countries were used by Israel to persuade their governments to intercede on behalf of Jewish communities in distress in other countries. The exodus of Jews from the U.S.S.R. is a well known, though by no means the only, example.

Finally, the existence of Israel undoubtedly influences the decisions of governments considering policies affecting the welfare, safety and rights of their Jewish residents. The existence of the State thus creates a situation in which the actual or contemplated persecution of Jews ceases to be a purely internal matter even for powerful countries.

The instruments of sovereignty are denied to other Jewish communities regardless of how well organized, politically powerful or rich they may be. But to live under Jewish sovereignty the Jews of Israel pay a heavy price. Until the peace with Egypt, all Arab countries rejected the existence of a Jewish state. Israel has therefore been forced, since her establishment, to fight four wars for her survival. Between hostilities, an alert defense posture must be maintained at all times. Consequently, Israelis serve three years (females, two years) in the regular army, and spend a month or more every year on reserve duty until they are fifty-five years old.

The economic costs of defense are enormous. They mounted in absolute and in relative terms until they exceeded one third of the gross national product following the Yom Kippur War. Thus, Israelis pay a high price for their sovereignty in terms of their physical security and their standard of living. This is much lower than it could have been, had they been able to spend less on defense and more on education, investment and the production of socially useful goods and services.

To live under Jewish sovereignty, Israelis must accept an additional constraint — they must give up what might be termed the historic Jewish occupational structure. In the free Diaspora, Jews have gravitated in relatively high proportions, as they did in earlier times when they were permitted to do so, towards self-employment in trade and commerce, and to the professions, academia and the arts. In Israel, the Jewish occupational structure must conform to the balanced requirements of the economy for workers in agriculture, manufacturing, transportation and communications and all other fields, and at all levels. In this, to be sure, they do not differ from workers in other lands. But their opportunities for upward mobility in the occupations traditionally favored by Jews are certainly more circumscribed than are those of Jews living in the free Diaspora.

Jews living in the democratic countries face different kinds of problems. They are usually well integrated into their host countries. They enjoy equal rights and obligations with their fellow citizens. Overt discrimination is uncommon and is likely to be frowned upon in private as well as in public. They can, if they so choose, live in closely-knit communities, send their children to parochial schools, and be relatively uninfluenced by their surroundings. If they choose otherwise, as almost all do, they can be involved in their communities and in the national affairs of their host countries. They often occupy positions of leadership and influence in their professions, in business, and in local and central government.

Their problem as Jews concerns the nature and extent of their Jewish affiliation, involvement and commitment. The choice they must make, moreover, is not a one-time necessity. It must be confronted repeatedly: in childhood, when playmates and a school are selected; when a spouse is chosen; when children are born; and again when Israel or another Jewish community is threatened. For most the choices are easy, taken almost for granted. For others, they are difficult, requiring each time a new affirmation of faith, a new evaluation of beliefs, values and habits, and confrontation with new challenges and burdens.

Experience has shown that when such choices must be made, the Jewish aspect tends to carry less and less weight as a function of time and of the degree of liberalism characterizing the communities in which Jews live. Thus, in the democracies, more and more individual Jews opt for general rather than Jewish education, for intermarriage, for more involvement in "general" and less in "parochial" concerns. This gives rise to the unfortunate contradiction between the "welfare of the Jews" and the "welfare of Jewry," a contradiction familiar from nineteenth century Europe: the better off the Jews are as individuals, the less they tend to be concerned with their "Jewishness."

There are, of course, many variations from the trend described above. Individual countries and communities display idiosyncracies which either contradict the trend or hasten it, but these do not change the overall picture. Concern for and involvement in Israel on the one hand, and revival of interest in religion on the other, appear to be the only factors capable of slowing or reversing this trend which, in combination with low and declining birth rates and a low rate of family formation among Diaspora Jews, has been described as "a demographic crisis."

Of the three groups, Jews living under dictatorships and totalitarian regimes such as the Soviet Union are undoubtedly the worst off. Despite the relatively large number of Jews among the leaders of the Bolshevik Revolution, Jews soon found themselves persecuted, first as individuals and later as members of a suspect and essentially alien group. They did not fare much better in other Communist countries. While the practice of religion and other forms of communal identification are actively discouraged, the way to individual "escape" via total assimilation is often hampered by both formal and informal barriers.

Totalitarian regimes by definition cannot tolerate nonconformity or dissent. The loyalty of Jews, who tend to be different, is therefore suspect. This suspicion is heightened by their relations with the outside world. Jews find it increasingly difficult to find jobs commensurate with their abilities and training. Fewer and fewer are admitted into the universities, either as faculty members or as students. It is not surprising that many Jews seek to leave and find a new life elsewhere.

To better understand the relationship among the three major community groups, we should consider their origins and the major composition of their membership.

Of the three groups, Israeli Jews and most of the Jews living in the democracies are of relatively recent origin. They consist largely of immigrants, and the children and grandchildren of immigrants.

Jews living in the totalitarian countries belong by contrast to long established communities which had been in the process of being voluntarily evacuated for many years preceding the Holocaust. The large Jewish communities of Eastern Europe, while growing in absolute numbers due to a very high reproduction rate throughout the nineteenth century, provided through emigration the bulk of the membership of the Jewish communities of the New World during the century preceding the Second World War. This emigration, though motivated largely by both economic and communal distress, was entirely voluntary. Jews were not forced to leave Poland or Russia. Those who left went in voluntary search of a better, freer, more equitable life elsewhere. Although millions left their homelands, other millions stayed behind.

Only a small proportion of those emigrants chose Palestine as their destination. The bulk went westward to America, while others went to Western Europe, Latin America and elsewhere. Those who emigrated to Palestine did so in the belief that Jews must have their own homeland. They subscribed to the Zionist view which held that, due to growing anti-Semitism and nationalism in the host countries, a continued and secure Jewish existence could be assured only in a country of their own. They maintained also that Jews must become a normal people, and that normalcy required a total transformation of Jewish life, including that of the traditional occupational structure. But those who preached and practiced the return to Palestine, it should be repeated, were only a tiny proportion of those who left Europe before World War II.

The Zionist view of the Jewish predicament proved all too accurate, as far as European Jewry was concerned. The slaughter of six million European Jews by the Nazis demonstrated what can happen to a people who are dehumanized by their host countries.

The establishment of Israel in 1948 came too late to save the six million victims of the Holocaust. It did however come in time to provide a haven for the Holocaust's survivors. The country's population was further increased by large numbers of other refugees from Arab lands. These people were driven from their homelands following the growing hostility of Moslems in general, and of the Arabs in particular, to the establishment of a Jewish state in the Middle East on a territory the Arabs regarded as theirs.

There is, then, a basic difference between the origin and composition of the three major groups of Jewish communities. Those who live in the totalitarian states stem from the old established communities which made up the majority of world Jewry in past centuries. These communities, which provided the reservoir of immigrants to both Palestine and the New World, had been declining in relative importance for decades and were decimated during the Holocaust. They are constrained by political, social and economic restrictions and their numbers are declining due to emigration, low reproduction rates and assimilation.

Jews in the democracies consist mostly of the progeny of immigrants who came to their new homelands within the last century, by free choice. While many Jewish communities in Western Europe were established centuries ago, they are vastly outnumbered by these more recent immigrants. They too are characterized by low reproduction and high assimilation rates. Their numbers may decline substantially in the coming decades, unless these trends are reversed.

And finally, the Israeli Jews, most of whom are refugees or the children of refugees. This refugee population was grafted onto a base organized and led by pioneers who came to the country voluntarily, who subscribed to the Zionist ideology and who were determined to bring about the establishment of a sovereign Jewish state. Note that most Jews who came to Palestine and later Israel voluntarily, i.e., not as refugees, were from East European countries which were, on the whole, inhospitable to their Jews. Relatively few came from Western Europe or America. Predictions based on recent reproduction rates suggest that Israel's Jewish population will continue to grow regardless of the immigration rate.

This background picture we have drawn of the composition of the world's Jewish communities suggests that the migration of Jews (as of other peoples) is motivated both by rejection and by attraction. These push and pull factors operate simultaneously. To leave one's country of birth one must feel rejected in some sense. When entire communities migrate their sense of rejection must be extremely strong. The choice of destination is affected by the alternative attractions held out to the migrant. Before the establishment of Israel, most Jews who were persuaded or compelled to leave their homelands demonstrated their preference for the Western countries over Palestine. This preference was ascribed to the superior economic opportunities and physical security offered by the West, on the one hand, and to the inimical policies in Palestine of the Turkish and later the British governments, on the other.

The establishment of the State in 1948 changed that last condition. Israel opened her gates to Jews from all countries and did indeed absorb about one and a half million immigrants. The large majority of these, however, were refugees who had nowhere else to go. Of those who had a choice, the majority chose the Western democracies. This is most clearly demonstrated by the current destinations of the emigrants from the U.S.S.R., as it was earlier by that of the emigrants from Algeria. Similar patterns have been also exhibited by recent Jewish emigrants from South Africa, Iran and Latin America. When Jewish emigrants have the choice, they recoil from the high taxes, the long army service, the threat of wars, the relatively low standard of living and of public services, and the much greater competition for jobs in the traditional Jewish occupational structure. The attractions of life under Jewish sovereignty have not been sufficiently strong to outweigh those offered by the more secure and prosperous Western democracies.

*Chapter Four*

# Israel

In her slightly more than three decades of existence, Israel has achieved many notable and impressive successes. She has successfully repelled, against great odds, repeated attacks on her existence. She has settled and developed a largely barren country. She has welcomed and absorbed more than twice as many Jews from all over the world as populated the country when the State was created in 1948, and succeeded in providing them with housing, employment and social services within a remarkably short period of time. All this was made possible only by an outstandingly high rate of economic growth and development in all economic and social sectors. Israel has provided millions of Diaspora Jews with a heightened sense of Jewish identity, enhanced their pride and self-respect, and gained for them a greater measure of respect from their non-Jewish fellow citizens. These contributions have been reflected in the close ties Israel has forged with the Diaspora, and in the mobilization of Diaspora financial, moral and political support for Israel.

Despite repeated wars and continuous siege, Israel accelerated the agrarian progress of the pre-state settlers, and developed a highly productive agriculture on largely reclaimed lands. She has developed an important industrial sector, a significant part of it highly sophisticated, technologically, and export competitive. She has achieved a high order of educational, scientific and cultural progress, and near-Western living standards. Zionist and socialist ideals found expression in important institutional innovations like the kibbutz, the moshav and the social ownership, through the trade union movement, of many economic enterprises, and created, especially in the earlier years, a spirit of humane egalitarianism. Israel also provided substantial technical assistance to many developing countries. Yet, in spite of these and many other notable achievements which require no recapitulation here, Israel today — quite apart from the vital problems of peace and security — is a troubled, anxious and demoralized society, beset with major and divisive economic, social and political problems she has not been able to find the way or the will to solve.

Of the key economic problems now confronting Israel, virulent inflation, the huge and widening balance of payments gap and the enormous public debt and external debt service burden stand in the forefront and reflect many others — most notably, the fundamental underlying problem of too low productivity in most economic and public service activities. Because of the close interrelation between inflation and other major economic problems, including the imbalance of payments and indebtedness, and also because inflation plays so large a role in Israel's most pressing social and even political problems, we shall concentrate here on the problems of inflation. But because we do not wish this statement to be regarded as politically tendentious, we emphasize that, in our view, previous governments share with the present government responsibility for the present state of Israel's economy.

The modern world has witnessed many aggravated national inflationary experiences. It is not necessary to document here their pervasive, debilitating, pernicious and ultimately devastating effects, if permitted to run their full course. Neither is it necessary to elaborate in detail on the morphology of this virulent economic and social disease currently afflicting Israel. Let it suffice to underscore that inflation in Israel has recently been growing at an annual rate well in excess of 100 per cent, that it is inimical to savings, investment, productivity and social morale; that it sets economic group against economic group as each tries to protect itself at the cost of others; that it encourages speculation and unnecessary anticipatory buying; that it creates largely illusory profits, and distorts rational resource allocation and use; that it erodes not only the faith of the society in the money issued by the government, but faith in the institution of government itself, progressively reducing the ability of the (or any) government to govern, and threatening the image and effectiveness of Israel in the world arena and, ultimately, the stability and viability of democratic Israel itself.

While some of inflation's worst effects have seemingly been offset in large part by indexing or linkage of wages and savings to the cost of living or to the dollar, such linkages cannot protect most wages and savings indefinitely. The huge defense outlays and public deficits which are largely responsible for the inflation also magnify the balance of payments deficit and require ever-larger foreign borrowing by the government, which has now reached a total of some $16 billion. If present trends are permitted to continue, the burden of servicing this ever-growing foreign debt will become intolerable. As the cost of servicing the foreign debt rapidly approaches the total flow of external resources (gifts and borrowing) that can be mobilized, very sharp reductions in both private and public consumption would become unavoidable. The entire financial structure based on external supports could collapse. The very economic foundations of the country would be seriously threatened.

Within this general picture, it is also necessary to note that previously operative inflationary pressures and trends have been increased by the cost of military redeployment in the Negev and by ever higher energy costs. It should also be clear that continued inflation will seriously endanger the potentially significant economic benefits which peace with Egypt might bring, after the redeployment has been completed, and the potentially great economic benefits of a more general peace. Only if Israel puts her economic house in order will she be able to reap the harvest that peace would make possible, promote more effectively the immigration she desires, keep her own young and talented people from emigrating, and provide to the Jews of the Diaspora the inspiration they can derive only from the existence of a secure, viable and socially healthy Jewish state.

In the forefront of a number of important socio-economic problems interrelated with inflation and with one another is that of the strained relations between Western or European (Ashkenazi) Jews and Asian-African ("oriental" or Sephardi) Jews. Many of the latter were relative late comers on the Israeli scene. For the most part, they were poorly educated, possessed of little or no capital and lacking in marketable skills. They were distinguished also by a different culture and language. Not surprisingly, in Israel they gravitated for the most part to low pay, low status occupations and, with their large families, into crowded living quarters, many of them in slums.

With their high birth rate, these Jews of North African and Asian origin now comprise some 60 percent of Israel's Jewish population. They have become increasingly sensitive to their relatively low status-low income occupations, larger than proportionate share in the poverty population and crowded slum housing, and to the limited upward mobility they have been able to achieve, not only economically, but socially and politically as well. In a setting where ready access and favorable consideration for jobs, promotions, housing allocations, loans and other needs within the control of the bureaucracy were importantly influenced by personal acquaintance and contacts with governments or quasi-public officials, the Sephardi felt keenly that they were not "members of the club," and were consequently denied the "protektsia" more readily available to Ashkenazi Jews. These cleavages and resentments, it became evident in the elections of 1977, took a political turn as these groups turned away in large numbers from their traditional support of the Labor party and supported Menachem Begin's Herut party instead.

It may be that the problem is more economic than ethnic. With time, schooling, acculturation and recognition of the problem, cleavages have begun to narrow and upward mobility in all fields has become increasingly eivdent. But recent polls indicating that many Sephardi Jews have turned away from their short-lived support of the present government suggest that their feelings of resentment remain strong and that much remains to be done. Disappointment over the slow start-up and limited progress on "Project Renewal," which held out high hopes for housing and slum renewal in largely Sephardi neighborhoods, has undoubtedly contributed to the strong feelings of the Sephardi community.

Housing has always been a problem in Israel. In recent years, the problem has become acute. Very short supply, sky-rocketing prices beyond the reach of all except the well-to-do, and the virtual non-availability of rental units at affordable prices are key aspects of the problem. Those most dramatically affected are the 25,000 or so new young couples each year who, having completed their army service and education, desire to set up their own homes and start family life. The impact is also severe on large families crammed into small quarters and on slum dwellers whose housing is far below acceptable standards. It is felt as well by families who, in order to meet their pressing housing needs, have undertaken loan or rent responsibilities well beyond their means. From another perspective, the extremely tight and costly housing market prevents the labor mobility the country sorely needs, if workers are to move from less productive to more productive occupations. Finally, there are indications that inability to obtain suitable and affordable housing has been a significant factor in the much deplored and resented decision by many young Israelis to leave the country.

In view of the multiplicity and magnitude of claims on Israel's scarce resources, it is plain that some limitations must be placed on the resources made available for housing. But the very large involvement of the government and its agencies, of the political parties and of the Histadruth in the housing field, and the abundance of complaints about their respective operations, suggest that there must also exist considerable room for improvement, all the way from the control and prices charged for land to the design, construction costs and distribution of the housing itself.

The case of Project Renewal, a special program of unique interest to Diaspora Jewry, is *apropos*. Unveiled in 1977, the plan called for $1.35 billion (later adjusted to $1.2 billion) to be contributed equally by Diaspora Jews and the government of Israel over the next four years to finance decent new homes and living conditions for some 45,000 families in 160 slum neighborhoods. The new housing would be central to neighborhood renewal programs that would embrace schools, community centers and other facilities, and required social services. The neighborhood people themselves were to participate actively in the actual planning. Individual Diaspora communities were to "adopt" individual neighborhoods and cooperate directly with them in preparing and implementing their plans. The Jewish Agency, local and municipal authorities and the Housing Ministry and other government agencies were, however, also to play key roles. Direct participation by those to be benefited by the project, and direct "twin" links between them and individual Diaspora communities, were novel and desirable innovations. But the cumbersome involvement of the several bureaucratic organizational layers called for by the plan, the complicated and time-consuming procedures established, and the differences in view and jurisdictional rivalries inevitably involved, have resulted in three years of gestation, little construction, much Government-Jewish Agency and intra-government disputation, blame and counterblame, and much Diaspora and neighborhood disappointment. Encouraging visible physical progress has begun to emerge in a number of neighborhoods, however, as in the Amistav quarter of Petah Tikva and the Neva Israel quarter of Herzliyah. If this momentum grows dynamically, early disappointments may soon be forgotten, and Project Renewal may before long blossom into an impressive demonstration of intimate Israel-Diaspora collaboration and make a major contribution to the health of Israel's society.

Project Renewal is also breaking new paths in the planning, administration and use of Diaspora aid to Israel. Typically, the Diaspora role in financial aid to Israel has concentrated on the raising of aid funds. Responsibility for the administration and use of these funds has been left to the Jewish Agency and Israeli department heads. Diaspora representatives have generally been reluctant to exercise their rights to participate in shaping the policies under which aid funds were to be administered. Project Renewal has been unique in that, for the first time, individual local communities in Israel, and individual local communities in the Diaspora, have participated directly in the planning and implementation of these projects in Israel, and in that they have "twinned" for this purpose in one-to-one relationships. This decentralization has provided Diaspora communities with greater voice in aid fund use, and with greater motivation and personal involvement. It has done the same for the neighborhood communities in Israel. Perhaps even more important, it has brought many more Diaspora and Israeli Jews into direct and cooperative working relationships, improving their understanding and communications with one another. These new departures will no doubt be suggestive of analagous approaches practicable in other problem areas and projects. Such an outcome, we feel, should be welcomed and nourished. We see this path as one which would lead to a far closer and deeper involvement by many more Diaspora Jews in the life of Israel, one which would at the same time enrich and reward their sense of Jewish identity and of Jewish living. It is also a path which could constructively lead many more Diaspora Jews to *aliyah*.

Religion has always been a problem in Israel, due to sharp differences between a relatively small, highly orthodox and activist minority and the relatively secular majority in the Jewish population. These differences have frequently erupted in violence of the stone-throwing variety, as in the case of vehicles driven on the Sabbath. More significantly, these differences have become intensified and taken a new direction in connection with West Bank autonomy negotiations and settlements policy. The differences have now become politicized, as exemplified in the Gush Emunim-Peace Now confrontation. To these strained religious divisions, one more must be added — that between the Orthodox rabbinate on the one hand, and the Conservative and Reform rabbinates on the other — a division which extends to their Diaspora peers. Because the Orthodox have been politically organized, and their party support has been essential to the life of successive coalition governments, they have been able to arrogate to themselves the sole right to declare who is a Jew, and to officiate at marriages, funerals, conversions and other basic ceremonies. These religious cleavages within the Jewish faith, in a Jewish State, add significantly to strains within the society. They have disturbing implications also for Israel's relations with the Diaspora — a matter to which we shall turn presently.

The problem of Israel's half million or so Arab minority seldom enters into the public discourse, perhaps because it is neither highly visible nor widely perceived to be a present one. But it is none the less important for all that, and it is bound to become increasingly so with the passage of time.

Israel's Arab are concentrated largely in three areas of the country, mostly in the Galilee. Lacking land for the expansion of agriculture, their traditional occupation, and lacking also Arab enterprises and institutions in their own localities which could provide them with employment and stimulate area development, the men typically commute to work in Jewish towns and enterprises by day, returning to their villages at night. Lacking seniority on these jobs, they tend to be the first fired, as well as the last hired. Moreover, since it is the Jewish Agency operating with contributed Diaspora funds, and not the government, which has been assigned the responsibility for rural settlements and their economic development, Arab villages have received no Jewish, and little governmental, development assistance. The Arabs live then in undeveloped rural enclaves, separated from the general society except for the daily work they do in Jewish communities.

Their income and living standards, to be sure, are substantially better than they had been before, although there has been little improvement in their housing or village facilities and services. Their most important advance has been in the schooling of their children, and the higher education of many. But teaching in the public Arab schools has been the chief occupational outlet for educated Arabs, except for some clerical jobs and employment in the Arab departments of government ministries and quasi-public agencies, while others have emigrated in search of better employment opportunities.

For many years, Israel's Arabs were politically quiescent, as Arabs, due chiefly to their limited communications with one another, the clannish competitiveness of their village politics and the cooptation of their elite in government employment. Their political protest took the form of support for Rakah, the Communist party, rather than of Arab causes as such. This situation has begun to change, as evidenced in the coordination of Arab student groups at Israeli universities. Support for the P.L.O. and for the creation of an independent Palestinian state on the West Bank and in Gaza is strong, and may before long find more effective means of expression. West Bank-Gaza autonomy or a Palestinian entity might well give rise to demands for separation or similar autonomy in Israel's Arab areas. With a far higher birth rate and population growth than that of the Jewish population, the prospective shift in Israel's demographic composition raises serious questions in itself. Clearly, the peace building process requires that serious consideration be given to the concerns and problems of Israel's Arab minority.

Most of these problems are interrelated and give rise to others. Thus, in fighting inflation, cuts in government spending curtail services to the poor and assistance to already distressed muncipal finances, while the withdrawal of subsidies which held certain prices below free market levels now push price indices higher. The higher taxes needed to contain budget deficits breed evasion and resentment against those who are able to escape paying them. The housing shortage creates resentment against immigrants who are favored in the distribution of the scanty supply available. Duty free imports and income tax benefits for new immigrants have the same effect. The omnipresence of government regulation and intervention throughout the economy leads inevitably to favoritism ("protektsia"), and bitter feelings among those who lack access to it. And so it goes. All this had led to a serious deterioration in the social fabric. In the words of a prominent Israeli sociologist, there has been "a general weakening of most of the institutional frameworks of Israel's society. . It is very difficult to find common norms which are accepted and upheld." Not only a high level of crime, and increasing lawlessness, but also an uncommon degree of violence, in the form of strikes, sanctions, stone throwing, verbal abuse, sheer rudeness and the like, are testimony to this judgment. So is the incessant and bitter competition among economic groups seeking to protect or improve their living standards without regard to its costs or effects upon others. There is a pervasive sense that the government has lost control, and is incapable of coping constructively with these problems. More significantly, from a Jewish point of view, there is a general sense that the Jewish goals and values Zionists hoped would flourish in a Jewish state are in an advanced state of erosion and are in danger of being permanently lost.

These internal problems have not newly emerged. Rather, they have accumulated and grown over a period of many years, and under successive governments, as a result of factors which, in some cases, go back to the earliest days of the State. They are therefore deeply rooted. Any attempt to deal constructively with the major elements of Israel's current malaise will have to take these underlying historical factors into account, and try to deal with them. Ironically, some of these factors are the very elements which have contributed so mightily in the past to Israel's greatest achievements and successes. It is thus the inadvertent maleffects of these elements, and especially, how they have contributed to low productivity in the economy — the other side of the coin, so to speak — to which we now turn our attention.

## The Ideology and Idealism of the Founders

Israel's founders were Zionists and social democrats with strong near-collectivist, egalitarian drives. They were idealistic, courageous men of strong will and undaunted spirit. Comradely relationships, communal sharing, and good pay and job security for workers were naturally high priority goals. These were reflected most notably in the agricultural collectives, in the work rules, social benefits and economic enterprises established by the trade union movement and in the personal austerity of the leadership. Social justice, in the early years, was a vibrant reality. Capitalism and the profit motive were naturally denigrated.

In practice, however, this had the effect, over time and with growing urbanization and industrialization, of also denigrating the need for productive efficiency, and obscured the terribly important fact that productive efficiency is as essential to a cooperative or to a socialist society as it is to a capitalist one. Among the consequences of this misunderstanding, over time, have been the neglect of basic economic principles and the misallocation and misuse of scarce resources. Worker pay levels were for a long time substantially divorced from productivity considerations. Workers' job tenure was considered more important than their job performance or the real economic benefit to the society of the enterprises in which they worked. Excessive

[53]

staffing and inefficiency in the public services increased the cost of government, contributed to budget deficits and diverted manpower from more productive occupations. The management function was also downgraded. Social outlook and party loyalties rather than management ability were for a long time the chief criteria of management selection in social organizations and socially-owned enterprises which accounted for a large share of economic activity. In consequence, inefficient workers, managers and enterprises were "protected" at the cost of the economy and the society as a whole. Despite significant improvements, especially in the export sector, these conditions persist in substantial degree today.

## *Aliyah and Early Industrialization*

The immigration of more than 1.5 million Jews, especially heavy during the earliest years of the State, imposed enormous challenges and problems of assimilation. Few came with significant resources, entrepreneurial experience or modern skills. Many were aged or in poor health. Many came from culturally deprived backgrounds and with little education. The need to settle, house and provide productive employment for those able to work was urgent.

Limitations on the availability of agricultural land, water supplies and other natural resources required Israel to concentrate on rapid industrialization to create employment opportunities for her fast growing labor force. Industrialization moreover was the path to a modern economy and the rising living standards which were deemed necessary to attract immigration from Diaspora communities in the economically advanced nations. A number of factors dictated the nature of the early stages of this industrial development.

The scarcities of capital, entrepreneurial experience and modern industrial skills, the small size of the domestic market, the inability at that time to seek to compete in international export markets, and the urgency of putting people to work quickly, many of them in new settlements, all mandated that the industrialization begin mostly with small, light and labor-intensive consumers goods industries in such traditional and import-substituting fields as foods and beverages, textiles, clothing, leather, and wood and paper products. Entrepreneurs needed and received considerable assistance from the government, chiefly in financing their enterprises, and in tariff and other forms of protection against imports which otherwise would have undersold them. Since each job created in manufacturing industry stimulated complementary employment in construction, transport, communications, energy, housing, financial and other services, and so on, this strategy was remarkably successful in fulfilling its primary task of fast job creation. It also provided needed training for the labor force, developed entrepreneurial and managerial experience and know-how, and supported the early stages of a scientific and technological research capability. But it had many deleterious effects as well.

The manufacturing industry which was thus developed was generally characterized, as of the mid-1960's, by a multiplicity of small, inefficient, high cost firms, with many products, sizes and costly small production runs, oriented to a small domestic market, with little internal competition and almost none from imported goods. It was characterized further by a heavy burden of both long and short term debt at high rates of interest, and hampered in the efficiency of its operations by an excessive trade union paternalism which made it difficult, if not impossible, for management to shift workers from one task to another or to discipline or discharge unsatisfactory workers. The extensive and complex degree of government intervention and controls caused many employers to spend more time in the corridors of government offices seeking relief or benefits than they spent in their own factories seeking more efficient operations or product improvement.

Other factors also entered into this picture. The urgent need for haste in job creation led inescapably to more than a few faulty *ad hoc* investment decisions that would have been avoidable in more normal circumstances. Security and other policy considerations sometimes required factory locations which were not the most economic. And in the public and quasi-public manufacturing sector, as previously noted, profitability was not in those years a clearly-defined or major objective.

With the 1960's, appreciation grew of the need for a new industrial strategy. This received a special impetus from the developments following the 1967 War, when Israel was forced to produce a considerable proportion of her defense requirements domestically. This set the stage for the creation of modern, efficient and internationally competitive export industries, and for the transfer to them of manpower and other resources from older, small scale, traditional and inefficient industries and firms. Government policy placed increasing emphasis on encouraging direct foreign investment and on encouraging and assisting both new firms and those older firms capable and interested in expanding their capacity to enter export markets. This policy has scored many notable successes. Production, employment and exports have grown rapidly in many modern and high technology industrial branches — electrical and electronic equipment, transport equipment, metal products and machinery, and chemical and oil products among them. Industrial exports played the dominant role in the ten-fold increase in Israel's exports from 1965 to 1978. This was a magnificent achievement. But it was hampered by the limited manpower available to the modern industrial sector. Rather than drawing manpower and other resources from the older, inefficient industries and firms, and from the excessively-staffed public services, it developed side by side with them. The relatively limited participation of females in the Israeli labor force constituted a further and significant work force constraint.

The dual nature of Israel's current industrial sector may be illustrated by a few key figures. As of 1978, little Israel had some 11.5 thousand manufacturing establishments employing 290,000 workers — an average of 25 workers per establishment. Only 167 establishments, or 1.5 percent of the total, employed 300 or more workers. Another 322 establishments, or 2.8 percent of the total, employed from 100 to 299 workers. These two groups, 4.3 percent of the total, accounted for nearly three-fifths of all manufacturing employment. At the other end of the size scale, two-thirds of all industrial establishments, employing fewer than 10 workers each, accounted for only 11 percent of manufacturing employment, and another 14 percent of all industrial establishments, employing from 10 to 19 workers, accounted for 7.6 percent of industrial employment. It would seem clear that many, if not most, of the workers employed in firms employing fewer than 50 workers — roughly one-third of the manufacturing labor force — are employed in firms too small to be competitively efficient.

On the ownership side, the continuation of small-scale, inefficient manufacturing enterprises reflects importantly both inertia and the attractive profit margins to be earned in the still-sheltered domestic market. On the government side, it reflects internal policy inconsistencies. The desire for exports and the much discussed need for the transfer of workers from less productive to more productive occupations have been counter-balanced by fears of small plant closings and even temporary unemployment.

## The Fight for Survival

The necessity to fight repeated wars for survival, and to maintain, between them, a constant state of readiness to repel renewed attack, has imposed enormous burdens on Israel's economy and society. Inescapable defense costs have contributed mightily to huge budget and balance of payments deficits, and to accelerating inflation. Due to rapid growth in the sophistication and cost of military technology, the accelerated and dangerous military build-up of her enemies, the declining value of the dollar and other factors, Israel's defense expenditures have taken over the years a rising proportion of her gross national product. During the 1950's and up to the 1967 War, defense costs accounted for roughly 10 percent of Israel's total output. (This compares with about 6 percent in the U.S. and lower percentages in Western Europe and Japan.) Following the Six Days War, this ratio increased to over 20 percent, and remained at about that level up to 1973. Following the Yom Kippur War, when the explosion of Arab oil revenues enabled Israel's adversaries to accelerate tremendously their rate of armanent, and the huge resulting balance of payments deficits of Western countries made them quite eager to seek military sales, still further and ever larger increases in defense expenditures were forced upon Israel. These rose to more than one-third of G.N.P. in 1975 and 1976, and have remained at about the 30 percent level ever since. In the absence of very substantial external assistance, such enormous diversions of domestically-generated resources would have been absolutely crushing to any economy, and would have made it impossible to meet to any extent the costs of economic development and immigrant absorption, let alone support existing living levels or permit gradual increases in them.

But however essential, there were certain resource diversions and impacts which external assistance could not supplant or compensate for. The scarce manpower engaged in active or reserve military service constituted a heavy drain on the economy. Managerial, technical and scientific talent were of necessity, and perhaps disproportionately, diverted to defense and defense-related activities. Careers were interrupted, or disrupted. Potential immigrants who might otherwise have come to Israel stayed away. Preoccupied with war, seige and international relationships, Israel's leaders were unable to deal adequately with many pressing domestic problems, or take time to plan effectively for emerging ones. War and siege, mistrust and suspicion, it has been pointed out, became a part of Israeli self-identity. This has made for an alienation vis-a-vis Israel's Arab minority, and contributes currently to the difficulties of the peace-building process.

### Reliance on External Assistance

External financial assistance from world Jewry, the U.S. Government, the Federal Republic of Germany (reparations and restitution payments) and other sources were absolutely essential, we pointed out, to help carry the crushing burdens imposed by Israel's defense needs. Part of U.S. official assistance went to meet military needs. The rest of it, and assistance from other sources, was used for immigrant absorption, economic development, social needs and other purposes which, in the absence a huge military budget, could have been met at least in part from Israel's own resources. One such purpose or effect has been to permit a steady rise through the years in the real income of Israel's people.

While external aid has thus been, and continues to be, of vital importance to Israel, the increasing reliance which has been placed on it has contributed to the creation of a psychology of dependence, and has operated through the years repeatedly to postpone into the indefinite future any serious attempt to come to grips with Israel's debilitating economic problems, or to forge the national will to achieve a greater measure of economic self-reliance. Once a psychology of dependence is permitted to develop, there tends to develop with it an expectation that errors or failures of judgment or policy or implementation never really have to be paid for by those who make them — because some external source can always be counted upon to bail them out of the mess. It would appear to be such expectations that have made it possible for successive governments in Israel to postpone or evade the necessity for hard, painful decisions — in Israel's case, the long evident and painful necessity to impose a certain degree of austerity, to limit borrowing against the future, and to achieve greater productivity and production by a combination of more realistic economic policies, better management and improved worker responsibility and effort.

## Modernization and Materialism

Israel's drive to modernize her economy has been spurred by her defense, employment and export needs, and by her desires to improve the living levels of her people and at the same time attract *aliyah* from Western Diaspora communities. We have already taken note of her remarkable achievements in industry, agriculture and other productive sectors, in science, education and technology, in social fields, and in institutional development. As in all other advanced societies, modernization has come at a price. It has brought with it a certain materialism and a growing number of personal discontents. These stand out more glaringly in the case of Israel because they contrast sharply with the idealism and egalitarianism of the early Zionists.

The extremely liberal incentives granted to stimulate industrial and other development and which included, till very recently, long term low interest capital loans unlinked to the rate of inflation, contributed to the creation of a new class of the rich and to a host of economic and social disparities and discontents. Rapidly growing income disparities were accompanied by a considerable degree of tax evasion and luxury consumption. The irritations arising out of housing, import and tax preferences accorded to immigrants were increased by supplementary incomes available to many of them from German restitution payments and other tax-exempt personal remittances from abroad. Such supplements further contributed to income disparities within Israel. Moreover, in view of the continuous devaluation of the local currency, such supplementary external income was not subject to the squeeze which inflation placed on Israelis dependent on incomes from domestic sources only.

Life styles, in the years before the State, had been quite simple — almost, one might say, Spartan. Moreover, the prevailing ideology, in those years, made a virtue of this necessity. With industrialization, and especially after the 1967 War, this gave way to rapid change. The acquisition of better housing and furniture, refrigerators and washing machines, automobiles and television sets became increasingly incorporated into the aspirations, and then into the expectations, of most Israeli families. These desires and expectations were naturally reflected in career and work preferences, attitudes and values. Professional and white collar occupations, which commanded higher status, higher pay and many untaxed perquisites, were ardently sought. Lower status and lower pay artisan and factory occupations were denigrated, limiting the labor available for factory employment, and impairing worker morale and productivity.

The growing materialism, and the individual and group competition for larger shares of those rewards it had to offer, hastened the erosion of the old idealism and the Jewish values — centering in the idea of social justice — it traditionally espoused.

## *Nationalism*

The existence of the State, pride in the new homeland and repeated wars and siege have inevitably, and desirably, fostered the development in Israel of one of the most powerful motivations in the modern world — the spirit of nationalism. The spirit of nationalism places primary emphasis on the promotion of the security, political, economic and other interests of the nation, as against those of all other nations or supranational groups. In the real world, these interests obviously cannot always coincide or be fully compatible with traditional Jewish values of peace, social justice and high ethical principles. Internally, moreover, these values suffered additionally from the inroads of modernization, materialism, individual and group competitiveness and consumer self-gratification as the idealism of earlier days weakened. With nationalism, therefore, Israel has become, increasingly, more like other nations, and less and less a *Jewish* state different in quality from all others.

This poses serious issues for the role of Israel in the world Jewish reality. Israel's ability to set an example for the Jewish communities of the Diaspora — of what being Jewish, and living a Jewish life, can and should mean — has become open to grave doubt and concern. Yet, because attachment and devotion to Israel have become central to the sense of Jewish identity for secular Jewry in the Diaspora, the importance of these bonds, which must rest heavily in the future on the quality of Jewish life in Israel, cannot be overstressed. We shall therefore return to this theme later in this report.

# Electoral System and Government Weakness

Israel's system of proportional representation was designed to assure legislative representation and political voice to even small minority groups within the polity. Election to the Knesseth is not by voters' choice among competing candidates within individual election districts, but by voting for competing party lists, with each party getting the number of seats, starting from the top of the list, which reflects each list's proportion of the total votes cast. This system obviously encourages the proliferation of political parties, and makes it very difficult for any single party to win a majority in the legislature. In Israel, the resulting multi-party system has given Israel a succession of coalition governments, whose effective action has been hampered by the practical necessity to compromise with even very small groups indispensible to the coalition, because their dissent and withdrawal from it at any time would cause the government to fall.

Such governments cannot avoid the tendency to compromise, or postpone, or avoid, the really basic controversial issues. They find it almost impossible directly to address and resolve them. The internal struggles and maneuvers which are inevitably involved in seeking the accommodation of group differences encourage the formation of cliques and constantly shifting alliances, an undue emphasis on narrow and special interests and an intensely factional, personal and unseemly kind of politics. Worst of all, the system conduces to weak and unstable governments. Responsible observers have had many occasions in the past to conclude that "Israel has no government." In such an institutional setting, how *could* difficult and basic issues be addressed and resolved?

If the foregoing analysis is reasonably correct, these several factors and their unintended maleffects have contributed importantly to Israel's current malaise. They have protected inefficiency in workers, managers and enterprises, distorted resource allocation and use, fostered an undue dependency on external donors and resources, heightened group divisions and tensions, eroded idealistic and Jewish values, weakened the will to face up to basic issues and diminished self-respect, confidence in government and confidence in the future. The inflation, the balance of payments gap, budgetary deficits and debt service burdens, frustrated expectations and weak economic policymaking all find much of their origins here. If this unhappy catalogue depicts the backdrop against which the drama of the possible consequences of peace must now unfold, it may also serve as a map outlining some of the lines along which Israel must begin to act if she is to put her economic and social house in order, so that the beckoning potentials of peace may constructively be realized.

## Chapter Five

# Jews in the Western Democracies

Of the approximately 10.6 million or so Jews who live outside Israel, about 7.3 million, or nearly 70 percent, live emancipated lives in the U.S., Canada, Western Europe, Australia and New Zealand — that is, in free, democratic societies where their rights of full citizenship are unquestioned, where they enjoy the full protection and security afforded by the law, and where they are (except perhaps by a "lunatic fringe") full accepted members of the national community.

For a long time Jews in these societies have been drifting away from orthodoxy to reform, and from Judaism and traditional Jewish practices — synagogue attendance, observation of dietary and other prescribed practices and marriage within the faith. Intermarriage and assimilation have been increasing for many decades, and the sense of Jewish identity had correspondingly been weakening steadily, until the Holocaust and the creation of the State of Israel. The Holocaust kindled in world Jewry a sense of participation in the fate of those who perished, a heightened sense of kinship and peoplehood. The creation of the State brought a new sense of elation, dignity, pride and hope. In the past three decades, Israel has served most Western Jews as a surrogate for the traditional Judaism from which they had strayed. Concern and support for Israel increasingly became the chief source and expression of their sense of Jewish identity. Fund raising, chiefly for Israel, and political activity to ensure the security and survival of Israel, have been the major activities of Jewish organizations during this period, especially in the United States.

This emphasis was only natural. The U.S. Jewish community is the largest, most politically active and potent, and possessed of the largest financial means. Further, the U.S. Government, primarily because of its own national interests and its dedication to the cause of democracy, but also because of the efforts of its Jewish population, had become by the 1970's Israel's major effective friend and protector on the international scene. The governments of Western Europe, with Jewish populations must smaller in relation to their population totals, and much more vulnerable to economic and political pressures by the Arab oil-producing nations, tilted significantly toward Arab demands for the resolution of their conflict with Israel. This climate was scarcely conducive to the same degree of vigorous and effective political efforts by the European Jewish communities on Israel's behalf.

American Jewry had achieved by the end of World War II sufficient acceptance by the general society to enable it to espouse the cause of Israel in the political arena without fears it might be accused of dual loyalty. European Jewry remained more sensitive to the possibility that it might be vulnerable to such a charge. Despite this, and their disinclination to act politically as Jews, the English, French and other European Jewish communities have protested vigorously to their governments from time to time against policies unfriendly or inimical to Israel — most recently, against policy declarations which threatened to subvert U.N. Resolution 242 and to promote the establishment of an independent Palestinian state under the control of the P.L.O. They have also reacted with dignity, courage and vigor to isolated terrorist actions by extremist groups.

Another significant difference among the Jewish communities in the democratic societies is also relevant here. Jews in the United States, and to perhaps a lesser extent the Jews in Canada and Australia, live in pluralistic societies side by side with many other groups of different national origins and cultures. In such a setting, cultural and religious differences are commonplace rather than unique. They are therefore not only much less marked; they are more likely to be generally tolerated and respected, if not indeed encouraged and even admired. Pressures to acculturate and assimilate are less pronounced in such a setting, and intermarriage often results in conversion of the non-Jewish spouse or in the adoption of Jewish "ways" by the non-Jewish partner and a strengthening of the Jewish identity of the other. In a significant proportion of cases where the non-Jewish spouse does not convert, the children are nevertheless raised in a Jewish atmosphere. In France, England, Germany, Italy, the Netherlands, Belgium and other European countries, where the national culture is not pluralistic but rather more homogeneous, the situation is quite different. The temptation, if not the pressure, for Jews to accommodate to the dominant cultural pattern is much more pronounced. In such countries, Jewish communities have tended to shrink, to be less strongly organized, and to become, by preference, much less active and less *visible*.

Of perhaps even greater importance than intermarriage and assimilation to the future of Jewish communities in the West in recent decades has been their characteristically low birth rates, due to greater sexual freedom, fewer and later marriages, more divorces, lower fertility and so on, and the resulting rise in the average age of the Jewish population. These trends signal, unless changed, a sharply declining Diaspora population in the future.

Within these broad currents, related (and sometimes counter) trends should be noted. The composition of some emancipated communities has been changed significantly by immigration — most substantially by the large influx of North African Jews into France, where they now comprise a large majority of the Jewish population, and in a lesser but still significant degree by Israeli, Soviet, Iranian and Latin-American Jews into the United States. In the United States, the indicated coming demographic decline of the overall Jewish community conceals the positive birth rate and prospective sizeable absolute growth of the Orthodox component of the community. If the much higher birthrate among Orthodox Jews should long continue, and if the children adhere to the ways of their parents, the proportion of Orthodox Jews within a declining total Jewish population would expand greatly. Orthodox Jews would in that case eventually become the dominant element within the American Jewish community. Of greater immediate significance is the fact that the membership of the mass Jewish organizations, especially that of the women's organizations, is on average quite elderly. In the case of the women's organizations, this reflects in part the very high percentage of younger women who have become members of the active labor force and who are therefore quite restricted in the time they can give to communal activities as presently organized.

Moreover, in the United States and in many other national Jewish communities, the last members of the earlier immigrant population are passing on. The predominant Jewish leadership passed some time ago from the rabbis, judges and other spiritual and intellectual leaders the older generation had followed. It is significant that earlier leaders of great influence like Louis Brandeis and Felix Frankfurter, Rabbi Abba Hillel Silver and Dr. Stephen R. Wise achieved such standing in the years prior to the establishment of the State of Israel. Since then, the real charisma in Jewish leadership has resided in Israel's leading figures. It is no accident perhaps that outstanding Diaspora leaders have more recently sometimes found themselves at odds with Israel's leaders, and became controversial figures in the Diaspora, as well as in Israel.

Diaspora leadership has passed for the most part, in other than religious organizations, to successful and wealthy businessmen of quite different characteristics and interests, who were capable of raising the huge sums needed by Israel and other Jewish communities in distress, and who enjoyed ready access to government leaders and policy-makers. More latterly, even this generation is beginning to pass on. Many of their sons and daughters have been turning increasingly, meanwhile, to the law, medicine, university teaching, research, the arts and intellectual pursuits in preference to the family business and the pursuit of wealth. Their interests and beliefs tend to be universalist and secular, rather than Judaic. Although many young Jews have become active in communal life, these generational changes raise serious questions about the future of Jewish leadership and the future of fundraising in the Diaspora for Jewish causes. The failure to seek or achieve the active involvement of more than a small minority of outstanding Jewish intellectuals in Jewish communal life has constituted a serious weakness which, unless remedied, may become even more serious in the future.

The great zeal of American Jews to serve Israel and other foreign and domestic communal purposes, and their responsiveness to a host of special purpose appeals, have resulted in a great outpouring of energies and means, channeled through a plethora of organizations into a myriad of constructive enterprises and accomplishments. In too many cases, however, these organizations are engaged in overlapping or duplicate activities which result in work lacking in depth and in the waste of communal resources necessarily scarce in relation to total needs. Perhaps the most seriously starved of vital communal needs, indirectly affected by such waste, has been that for Jewish education.

Since this discussion has sought to focus on trends of significance for the future, we should take note here of a seemingly emerging development which could take on great future importance. In the period following World War II, American Jewry made great strides in terms of general acceptance by the society, upward mobility, and of income, status and influence — especially political influence. All this has naturally been of enormous help to Israel's survival and welfare. But it may be that Jewish influence in America has already achieved and passed its peak, and that future years may witness its relative decline, due chiefly to the upward thrust and increasing relative influence of the much larger, rapidly growing and ever more assertive claims of the Black, Puerto Rican and Mexican-American communities, who feel very strongly that it is now their turn "to make it" in America. American Jewry will of course continue to be sympathetic and helpful to them in this effort, as it has always been in the past. But its own influence in the larger community, relative to theirs, may well decline.

The most important of the trends observable among Western and especially American Jewry in recent years, in our opinion, have been those involved in the relationship with Israel. The basic elements in this relationship, it should be affirmed, are clear and positive. For

Diaspora Jews, Israel serves, variously, as a source of identity, people-hood, pride and dignity; as a potential haven; as a spiritual center for some, a surrogate for Judaism — a secular religion, really — for others. For Israel, the emancipated Diaspora serves as a source of indispens-able economic, moral and political support; of keenly desired immigra-tion; of intellectual, scientific and technological resources. The inter-dependence of Israel and this Diaspora, the essentiality of each to the other, require no affirmation. The relationship is of inestimable value, and vital to both. This is why we are gravely concerned by the increas-ing strains which have become evident in the relationship in recent years.

We refer here to no ordinary strains. Some degree of strain would be quite inevitable and readily accommodated in a relationship as deep, rich and multi-faceted as this. But the strains that have been developing in the Israel-Diaspora relationship go far beyond the ordi-nary. Successive Israeli governments, self-centeredly, have taken the unquestioning support of the Diaspora for granted, all too often in cases where Israeli positions occasioned serious questions, doubts and even dissent in the minds of many Diaspora Jews. Yet the dependence of such Diaspora Jews on the Israel connection for their sense of Jew-ish identity, as well as their respect for Israel's leaders, has made it difficult for them, over the years, to express their doubts, criticism or dissent in such matters, for fear of injury to an irreplaceable bond. Nor was this the only operative constraint. Diaspora Jews who played active organizational leadership roles were conscious that such expressions in all probability would be neither understood nor accepted by their members, and that the warm welcomes to which they had been accus-tomed in Jerusalem might become cool or even chilly receptions. They have therefore mostly abstained, while frustration and discontent have accumulated. Their pressures have already created a number of visible leaks in that bond. We consider it essential therefore to bring these differences into the open so that pent-up pressures can be relieved, and constructive efforts can be made, through candid dialogue, to resolve them.

For reasons already stated, these differences, criticisms and frus-trations to which we shall now refer apply more to the American Jew-ish community than to any other, although they are not unique to American Jewry. To examine these in an orderly way, we shall address them in a framework which embraces the major economic, social, cul-tural, religious and political aspects of the relationship. We shall need to address also a number of specific problems which do not readily fall within these classifications, the most outstanding of which are immi-gration (*aliyah*), emigration (*yerida*), Soviet emigres "dropouts" (*neshira*) and the implications of concepts like "the centrality of Israel," "we are one" and "partnership."

[65]

On the economic side, the most obvious of the current questions have to do with how funds raised within the several Diaspora communities should be shared among Israel, other Jewish communities and the national communities concerned. It is recognized, to be sure, that Israel needs and is entitled to priority for the lion's share generally accorded her. It is also recognized that, where there is a joint appeal for funds, the residual remaining to the fund-raising Diaspora community is generally larger, *after* the allocation to Israel, than would have been the case had the community engaged in fund-raising for its own purposes alone. There is some feeling nevertheless that certain Diaspora needs, especially that for Jewish education, have seriously been neglected. Less obvious and less widely recognized are questions which arise out of the administration and use within Israel of the funds raised and allocated by the Diaspora. The Jewish Agency, which administers the utilization of these funds for immigration and absorption, settlements, education and social welfare, is politicized as to both direction and staff, reflecting at any given time the political party composition of the Israeli government and their respective priorities and nepotistic personnel interests. The disinclination or failure of Diaspora members of the Jewish Agency leadership to play a meaningful policy role, in the past, in its areas of assigned and legitimate responsibility has occasioned serious criticism from Israeli as well as Diaspora Jews. Some Israeli critics indeed go so far as to say, partly on this account, partly for other reasons, that the flow of Diaspora funds to Israel has in many ways been debilitating and counterproductive.

A third problem in the economic aspect of the relationship is the matter of the disappointingly small direct investment by Diaspora Jews in Israel, relative to their extremely generous contributions to fund-raising appeals. This calls for notice of a far more important matter. Knowledgeable Diaspora Jews have viewed Israel's economic management and policies over the years with increasing dismay and dissatisfaction. Successive Israeli governments have engaged for a long time in day-to-day crisis management of the country's economic affairs without regard to the longer-term implications of *ad hoc* emergency decisions hastily improvised in a crisis atmosphere, with the dire results visible today. Appeals for far greater direct business investment by Diaspora Jews, as distinct from purchases of Israel Government bonds, are quite unrealistic in a setting where grave concerns are felt for the future viability of Israel's economy and policy.

Another set of differences which need to be aired are concerned with social, cultural, religious and spiritual questions. One basic point of difference is that many, if not most, Israelis still seem to take the view that the Diaspora doesn't really *count* — that it has no real intrinsic worth apart from its connection and usefulness to Israel, that there is no significant prospect of a secure, real and independent Jewish exist-

[66]

ence in the Diaspora in the future. This indeed is the meaning of the term *aliyah* — emigration to Israel, by definition, is return and *uplift* from an insecure and diminishing Jewish future in exile (*galut*). But emancipated Jewry does not feel that it is living in exile, and secular Jews do not think of emigration to Israel as uplift or redemption. For these and other reasons previously mentioned, Israel's efforts over the years to promote *aliyah* from Diaspora communities in the West have been productive of disappointingly meager results. It is quite clear that Israel's perennial hopes and expectations with respect to such *aliyah* have not been realistic. Neither, in the opinion of some Diaspora observers, do they at present take into account such practical problems as the timeliness of current *aliyah* program efforts.

The other side of this coin is the increasingly troubling question of the large number of Israelis who have left Israel to live and work in the emancipated West — mostly in the United States. In Israel's terminology, they are *yordim* — the fallen. These now number anywhere from 350,000 to as many as 500,000, by some estimates — perhaps one for every six Israelis living in Israel. They create a difficult situation for Diaspora Jews, partly because of the *yordim's* own sense of embarrassment, and partly because Israel denigrates them and is embarrassed by the undiagnosed phenomenon they represent. Diaspora organizations have therefore not yet adopted a policy or posture with respect to them. But if these Israeli emigres now constitute some 6 percent of America's Jewish population — one out of every 16 or so Jews — some policy or posture must be developed. They simply cannot be ignored. And if so many of its own people have elected to leave Israel, should not Israel be asking itself some rather basic questions about the *why* of this phenomenon, its implications for the state of Israel's society, and its implications for *aliyah*?

Another difficulty for many Diaspora Jews has been their growing sense that raising funds for Israel, and seeking through political means to help maintain Israel's survival and security, are not sufficient in themselves to serve as a basis for an enduring and satisfying Jewish life. Also, while they may be glad to use themselves, or even to be used by Israel, for these purposes, they do not feel that these provide an adequate basis for a healthy and constructive Israel-Diaspora relationship. This leads us to an even more important point, namely, the disappointing perception on the part of many Diaspora Jews that Israel has failed to achieve and embody that special character which would enable it to serve as "the spiritual center for the majority of Jews who were living outside the Jewish state." The religious monopoly exercised by the Orthodox rabbinate in Israel with the official sanction of the government — a situation offensive to Conservative and Reform Jewry, as well as to many secular Jews, in the Diaspora — comprises only a small though significant part of this much broader problem.

The core of the political relationship between Israel and the Diaspora has of course been Diaspora support for Israel's security and assistance needs. This support has always been, and continues to be, ardent. But many Diaspora Jews nevertheless feel that Israel has always taken for granted the primacy of her own needs, interests and views, while those of the Diaspora communities have not been taken adequately into account, and have sometimes been completely ignored. Indeed, Diaspora Jews have often resented what they considered Israel's manipulation of the leadership, policies and activities of their own Diaspora organizations. They have resented even more what they considered Israel's occasional intrusions into their national politics and policies, sometimes to the community's detriment or embarrassment, and often without even consulting them. This has at times created difficulties of conscience or "exposure" for the communities.

Far more serious and disturbing than these have been the differences which arose over the negotiations with Egypt concerning autonomy for the West Bank and Gaza, and over Israel's settlement policy. In the view of many Diaspora leaders, the government of Israel has displayed an extremely parochial obtuseness in its lack of appreciation of the highly significant and increasingly critical public opinion in the U.S. and other Western nations with regard to these policies. Moreover, they resented that Israel not only ignored their doubts and disagreements with these policies, but expected them to suppress these and present a united front vis-a-vis their own governments in support of them. Finally, some Diaspora leaders close enough to be familiar with Israel's political scene are disturbed by its intensely fragmented, factional, personal, contentious, unstable and generally unseemly nature. All this has already led some to point out that the obligation of Diaspora Jews unfailingly to support Israel does not necessarily extend to the policies of any given Israeli government.

Some observers have attributed many of the differences and difficulties in the recent Israel-Diaspora relationship to "communications" problems. These problems are not however problems of language; they reflect rather important differences on basic ideological issues, bearing in mind always that the thinking within Israel and within the Diaspora communities on many key issues is exceedingly diverse. These ideological issues are succinctly embodied in certain code words and phrases which occur in or underly much of the current dialogue.

"The centrality of Israel" is such a phrase. To many Israeli spokesmen and to the official Zionist organizations, this is shorthand language for the chief tenets of classic Zionist ideology, as re-stated in the Jerusalem program of the World Zionist Organization. This embraces the recognition of Diaspora as exile, the need for an ingathering of exiles to Israel, and the affirmation of the primacy or centrality of

Israel for Jewish survival and self-determination. As understood in the free Diaspora, however, the centrality of Israel "does not mean that the Diaspora regards itself as in the process of building itself into the state. It means, on the contrary, that the labors for the state are the prime preservative of the Diaspora."

Another such phrase is "we are one." Both Israeli and Diaspora Jews agree that all Jews, wherever they may live, comprise one people. (One prominent Diaspora thinker has indeed argued the case for the "centrality of the Jewish people" rather than the "centrality of Israel.") For some Israeli leaders, however, the concept of peoplehood goes further. It has been used, for example, to suggest that there is no room, within this concept, for the kind of independent or separate thinking that underlies the introduction of "we" and "they" into the Israel-Diaspora dialogue, that all should be oneness and unity, especially where Israel is concerned. Many Diaspora leaders however regard the essential oneness and shared values of the Jewish people as quite compatible with the existence within it of distinct groups with obvious differences in their conditions, interests and views.

We may consider finally the disparate meanings attached to two code words frequently used in conjunction — "partnership" and "common agenda." For many Israelis, the "common agenda" of Israel and the Diaspora communities is not far removed from that implied by their own understanding of "the centrality of Israel." So, too, with the "partnership" concept. This was well illustrated in a recent address by an Israeli leader to an important Diaspora meeting. He referred in his introduction to the concensus reached by an international task force of Israeli and American Jews on four basic principles. The last of these read as follows: "There is a concensus that the Israeli and American Jewish communities share an agenda of common concerns that require reciprocal and mutual determination." Diaspora Jews naturally take the phrase "that require reciprocal and mutual determination" to represent the *partnership* component in the relationship. But when the Israeli leader came, later in his speech, to address the agenda of common concerns arising out of this concensus — essentially an Israel-centered agenda — he no longer found it necessary to recall or deal with the concept of "reciprocal and mutual determination." That aspect was not a live element in his thinking.

With this background, we return to the question of "the centrality of Israel." There can be no doubt that Israel will continue to play the central role in Jewish life. The need for Israel to provide physical and spiritual insurance for Diaspora Jews, to serve as a haven for those communities who find their existence threatened by external events or internal disintegration, to preserve, embody and renew Jewish traditions and values, to preserve Jewish history and revitalize Jewish culture, to provide a core with which Diaspora Jews can identify and sustain their Jewish consciousness — all these assure Israel's continued centrality. What may be in some doubt is the quality of that centrality and the closeness of the ties between that center and its periphery in the Diaspora. These will depend in major degree on Israel's success in coping with the social and economic problems with which we have been concerned — the need to combat inflation, resume economic growth, reduce the balance of payments deficit, reduce social and communal discord, improve the equity of income distribution, find a modus vivendi with the Arab minority within Israel and make progress towards a just and durable peace with the Arabs. They will also depend in major degree on the ability of Israel and the Diaspora to forge new and constructive links with one another based on spiritual, cultural, economic and family relations, to augment the old links so heavily based on the fund raising and political support needed to assist an infant state forced by its enemies to fight repeatedly for its physical survival. These tasks, so essential to the revitalization of the Jewish people in Israel and the Diaspora, can be accomplished only by a joint effort. The size and scope of this essential effort cannot be encompassed within the existing machinery for Israel-Diaspora communication and collaboration.

One source of deep frustration noted over the years by many thoughtful observers, both in Israel and the Diaspora, arises out of basic and inherent difficulties in devising an appropriate institutional structure and forum through which all the major problems in the relationship could be addressed and resolved. The functions of the Jewish Agency are limited to immigration and absorption, settlements, education and welfare in Israel. Even if current efforts to improve its functioning should prove to be successful, the Agency clearly cannot speak for the Diaspora on the broad range of Israel-Diaspora problems we have outlined. What organization or group then, and how selected, could represent and speak for the Diaspora? If such an organization or group could be devised (selected, constituted), could it engage in a symmetrical dialogue with a sovereign state? And further, what would be an appropriate scope of the subject matter for such a dialogue, and what limits, if any, should define and provide boundaries for such discussions? We must recognize that there may be many questions which either Israel or the Diaspora will wish to reserve for their own decision-making, or may not even be willing to discuss. But surely there should be a mutual willingness to discuss all common problems, and all matters where either Israel or the Diaspora perceive the need for joint action, or desire to turn to the other for counsel or help. Meanwhile, it seems appropriate to observe that these unresolved and pent-up problems, difficulties and frustrations threaten to demoralize Jewish leadership in the Diaspora. We consider the problem of devising an appropriate forum for a genuine dialogue to be of fundamental importance to the future of Israel-Diaspora relations.

*Chapter Six*

# Soviet and East European Jewry

Nearly a fifth of all world Jewry — about 2.5 million — live in the Soviet Union and its East European satellites. The great majority of these live in the Soviet Union. The next largest communities are those in Hungary (80,000) and Romania (for which estimates range from 35,000 to 45,000). Of the remaining communities, those in Czechoslovakia, Bulgaria and Poland are considerably smaller, and that in East Germany negligible in number. (The community in Yugoslavia, also quite small, is not included with the Soviet Bloc). We concentrate therefore here on the problems of Soviet Jewry, the third largest Jewish community in the world.*

Life in the Soviet Union for the Jewish people has continued in many essentials their life under the Czars. Jews suffered discrimination in pre-Soviet Russia, and occasional pogroms; but they were able to practice their religion. Under the Soviets, there have been no pogroms, and Jews have been able to achieve a high level of education and the occupational rewards to which that education has been the avenue. But anti-semitism has been pronounced, and the government has made it virtually impossible for Jews to practice their religion or to pass it on to their children.

Relatively few among the present generation of Russian Jews know anything about their religion. Their sense of Jewish identity is one that is forced upon them by the stamp on their identity cards and the discriminatory treatment to which they are subjected. Many have sought to assimilate and "disappear" as Jews, and succeeded. Others

---

*The most recent Soviet census (January, 1979) gives the Jewish population at 1,811,000. The decline of some 340,000 since the census of 1970, when the total was given at 2,151,000, is atrributed in almost equal part to emigration and natural causes. Estimates by the American Jewish Yearbook do not find the Soviet census credible, and place the Jewish population in 1978 at 2,666,000.

undoubtedly are in that process. The pressures of a totalitarian society which attacked "rootless cosmopolitans" (meaning Jews) viciously, then created the fanciful Jewish "doctors' plot" against them, and finally initiated a full-blown campaign against Zionist "capitalism-imperialism-racism" — a campaign which still continues, accompanied by a barrage of anti-semitic publications resembling those of Nazi Germany in their lies, hatred and filth — have made it almost mandatory for Jews to seek either to emigrate or disappear. Increasing difficulties imposed by the government on the entry of Jewish youth into the universities, and the rank discrimination introduced into qualifying entrance examinations, especially for doctoral degrees, have provided significant additional strength to emigration desires in recent years. So has the growth of a courageous Jewish dissident movement which has become quite outspoken. Many applicants for emigration have sought, while waiting, to improve their knowledge and understanding of Judaism.

Fortunately, and for a variety of reasons, the Soviet Union in recent years has opened the gates to Jewish emigration much wider than before. During the 1960's, it permitted only some 9,000 Jews to leave. During the 1970's this total swelled to over 220,000. In 1979 alone, more than 51,000 Jews were permitted to depart. Since the age mix of those departing was significantly younger than that of the Jewish population as a whole, and their sense of Jewish identity was presumably greater, the emigration pointed to a double acceleration in the declining size of the Jewish population in the Soviet Union — one for demographic reasons, the other because of a relatively greater propensity towards assimilation by the population remaining. Running counter to this last trend, however, would be the increased "pull" factor exerted by greater numbers of relatives and friends already outside the Soviet Union.

No dictatorship wishes to give its people the opportunity to prove, by "voting with their feet," that living conditions within its borders range from less than acceptable to the intolerable. Further, the granting of exit privileges to any one group makes it difficult to deny the same permission to others. The Soviet Union has sought to minimize these considerations by making Jewish emigration conditional on reunion with family members in Israel. This tied in also with the human rights obligations to which the Soviets subscribed in the Helsinki agreement. But the governing influences for this change in policy would seem to have been the desire of the Soviet Union to obtain "most-favored-nation" treatment in its trade relations with the United States, and the liberal credits, easier technology transfer, accord on a second SALT agreement and the general progress towards an (from their point of view) improved detente that would be likely to accompany most-favored-nation treatment. Other factors in this easement of emigration policy for Soviet Jewry during the 1970's may have been a desire to reduce the growing dissident "nuisance" and the Soviet's increasing ability — due to a higher proportion of non-Jewish university graduates — to staff with Russians many of the high-skilled, professional and high technology posts previously held by Jews.

Any assessment of Soviet Union motivations is, however, speculative; any forecasting of future Soviet policies, in this or any other regard, is even more so. In the first nine months of 1980, the number of Jews permitted to emigrate dropped by some 52 percent from the same period a year earlier — from 38,236 to 18,369. More ominous was the pace and trend of the decline, from close to 8,900 in the first quarter of 1980 to about 6,200 in the second quarter and to less than 3,300 in the third quarter. These represented progressive declines of 25 percent, 52 percent and 75 percent, respectively, from the same quarters of 1979. The drop early in 1980 was thought at first to reflect the sudden cooling in Soviet-U.S. relations that followed the Soviet military incursion into Afghanistan. Prompt American counter measures may indeed have been part of the reason for the more intensive scrutiny by Soviet authorities of Jewish applications for exit permits. Letters of application are being denied unless the letters of invitation from Israel come from immediate family members — spouses, parents, children and siblings — or when it is clear that close relatives who departed the Soviet Union earlier did not settle in Israel. There is evidence however that these new criteria were already being introduced in the months prior to the Afghanistan affair, and that they reflect therefore other considerations. Further, there has reportedly been a sizeable recent decline in requests by Soviet Jews for letters of invitation to be sent them from Israel. Whether this reflects a fear of the stigmatization and other consequences which might follow from application and its rejection, or a substantial diminution in the number of Soviet Jews still desirous of emigration, or still other reasons, is not clear. Neither can it be assumed, given Soviet unpredictability, that the recent decline in emigration will continue, or accelerate, or that it will not be reversed.

These imponderables and uncertainties bring us to a quite different and most difficult problem — that of Jewish policy with respect to the destination of the Soviet Jewish emigres. Leaving the Soviet Union with Israel visas based on affidavits supplied by Israeli relatives, the emigres arrive first in Vienna, where they are interviewed in the first instance by Jewish Agency representatives. If they opt at that time to proceed, not to Israel but to some other destination (for the most part, the U.S.), they are assisted to do so by the HIAS, which brings them to Rome for orientation assistance by HIAS, the American Joint Distribution Committee and the ORT before proceeding on their onward journey. On arrival, they are helped forward to the cities where Jewish community organizations have undertaken to receive and help them, financially and otherwise, in building new lives. What has been troubling, especially to Israel, is that a large and increasing proportion of Soviet Jewry has been choosing to go to destinations other than Israel. In 1976 and 1977, the "dropout" rate was about 50 percent. In 1978, this rose to 58 percent, and in 1979, to 66 percent. For the first nine months of 1980, the average dropout rate was little changed, although it rose to over 70 percent for the third quarter. But because prior to 1976 the great majority of emigres went to Israel, approximately 150,000 of the 220,000 Jews who left the Soviet Union during the 1970's now live in Israel.

The chief possibilities for major immigration to Israel in the foreseeable future lie with Soviet Jewry. The Israelis feel, understandably, that since it is they who provide the visas and the opportunity for Soviet Jews to leave, Soviet Jews should come to Israel, and accept the citizenship which is accorded them as a matter of right. Moreover, Israelis feel they cannot compete on even terms with the far greater material benefits and opportunites — and greater security — which beckon in the United States and other Western countries. They also believe that most Soviet Jews who settle in the West may soon be lost to Jewish communal life and Judaism, whereas those settling in Israel will be saved for Jewry. At the very least, they feel, the Soviet emigres should come to Israel in the first instance, for long enough to enable them to make an informed choice — they would of course always be free to leave thereafter, if they so chose. For all these reasons, they regret the active support which Diaspora organizations have accorded to the Soviet Jews who have elected to go to countries other than Israel — a support which includes transportation to Rome for orientation and preparation there, onward transportation to their countries of chosen destination and, in the United States at least, assistance in settlement, guidance, orientation, job seeking, and free Jewish education for their children. Most recently, the Israelis have stressed the point that Soviet Jewish emigres are not refugees, since they carry visas for their national homeland where they are welcome. They are therefore highly critical of the possible application to Soviet Jewish immigrants to Israel of U.S. legislation which accords them the privilege and benefits of refugee status in the U.S. for up to one full year after they have arrived in Israel. All this amounts, in the Israeli view, to unfair competition.

Israeli distress over this loss of a potential and keenly desired *aliyah*, and the prevailing view in the American Jewish community that Soviet Jews are entitled to make a free choice as to where they wish to live, and are entitled also to the active assistance of the community in getting to and settling in countries of their choice, constitute a basic difference which has not yet been resolved. There is no question, of course, in either Israel or the Diaspora that Jews desirous of leaving the Soviet Union should be helped to do so, or that those who remain there should be free of discrimination and free to practice their religion. Neither do the Israelis challenge the principle of freedom of choice as to country of destination, although they would strongly prefer this right to be exercised only after the emigres had had at least an initial exposure to Israel. The real issue is whether Soviet Jews should receive the active assistance of organized Jewry to settle in countries other than Israel.

Some American Jewish communities, to be sure, have already decided to withhold financial assistance to Soviet Jews after their arrival in the U.S., and to leave the burden of such assistance to relatives and friends of the emigres already resident in the country. The seeming indifference of many Soviet Jews to the efforts of the communities to integrate them into the body of Jewish organizations and communal life and the very considerable cost of these assistance programs, as well as Israel's expressed views, might well lead to substantial changes from the prevailing assistance policy.

We see no compelling logic in the position that adherence to the freedom of choice principle requires that active resettlement assistance be extended by organized Jewry to those who choose not to settle in Israel, although some distinction might well be made between financial help in getting to other countries, and assistance after arrival at those destinations. Assistance on a repayable loan rather than grant basis might also be considered. But it seems to us that other considerations are also important here. Housing, for example, is desperately short in Israel. If the number of immigrants from the Soviet Union (some 17,000 or so in 1979) had been doubled or tripled, how and where would they have been housed, and whose or what needs would have been denied to make this possible? Second, a significant proportion of Soviet emigres are highly educated and technically and professionally trained, many of them in fields of narrow sub-specialization for which opportunities in a small economy like Israel's are quite limited. This situation is aggravated now by the economic slowdown imposed by the government's anti-inflation measures, and increasing unemployment. Scarce and costly housing, and limited work and career opportunities, have contributed to an average annual emigration from Israel of 10,000 or more of her own citizens, of whom as many as perhaps 500,000 are now living abroad, most of them in the U.S. Would increased immigration from the Soviet Union result in even more Israelis leaving their own country, and if so, would such a cost be desirable or acceptable? It seems clear to us that the questions involved in the Soviet emigre issue go far beyond the simple terms in which the issue has till now been couched. Indeed, these latter questions come into play with respect to the broader question of *aliyah* from any source. On the other side of the coin however are the tougher criteria in reviewing exit applications invoked by the Soviet Union late in 1979. As long as Jewish applications for emigration are accepted only from those who have "first degree" relatives in Israel, those who leave such relatives behind and opt to settle in countries other than Israel effectively close the door to possible emigration by the relatives they leave behind. This restriction may of course not endure, and those left behind may never wish to leave the Soviet Union. Clearly, the decision is one only the individuals concerned can make. But this new situation constitutes nevertheless a strong argument in favor of sincere Diaspora cooperation with Israel in seeking to persuade as many Soviet Jewish emigres as possible to elect Israel as their destination.

## East European Jewry

We shall offer only a few brief observations on these communities which were so heavily decimated by the Holocaust, and which were later further reduced by substantial emigration to Israel through the 1950's. Their pre-war population of some 5 million now numbers perhaps 150,000.

In sharp contrast to the anti-semitism of the Soviet Union, Hungary and Romania have been much more tolerant. They permit Jews freely to practice their religion and even in some cases assist financially to support Jewish communal life. The communities are organized, have their own publications and cultural activities, and are officially recognized. Anti-semitic practices are illegal. Varying degrees of contact with world Jewry are permitted, as is a certain amount of foreign travel. Poland too is relatively tolerant. Czechoslovakia however has been anti-Zionist, anti-Israel and anti-semitic.

Due chiefly to the Holocaust, the Jewish communities of Eastern Europe are disproportionately elderly. In Romania, for example, more than 50 percent of the population is reported to be more than 60 years old. Although elderly Jews are mostly survivors of the Holocaust, little Yiddish or Hebrew is spoken. There are few teachers for the young, who for the most part show little interest in the faith of their fathers. All in all, it is difficult to be sanguine about the future of these Jewish communities which, only a few decades ago, accounted for a major portion of world Jewry.

## Chapter Seven

# Latin American Jewish communities

Close to 600,000 Jews live in Latin American countries — some 550,000 is South America, about 38,000 in Mexico and perhaps 11,000 in Central America and the West Indies. Argentina (300,000*), Brazil (130,000) and Uruguay (50,000) account for about 80 percent of the total. Mexico, Chile (28,000), Venezuela (17,000) and Colombia (14,000) are the next largest communities.

For the most part, Jews living in these well-organized communities are relatively well-to-do. The nations in which most of them live, however, are governed by military dictatorships and are characterized by a high degree of political, economic and social tensions and instabilities. Their military governments have reacted with severely repressive measures against the challenges of Leftist and violent guerilla movements, with little regard for democratic principles and human rights. While they are not, in general, openly anti-semitic, in most of these countries even native-born Jews are widely regarded as aliens. Since Jews comprise only small minorities in those countries, they are not feared and if some are persecuted, it is not because they are Jews, but rather because they are regarded as being in actual or potential opposition to the regime. But in at least one country, the right-wing response to Leftism does appear to have taken on a Nazi hue.

Politically, the climate in which most Latin American Jews find themselves is both awkward and delicate. Authoritarian government is not compatible with Jewish philosophy and values. Yet, since the more likely alternatives to these governments seem to be an even more authoritarian extremism of the Right or of the Left, Jewish organizations try to maintain politically neutral positions and show a low profile. This has created a serious relationship problem *visavis* their own youth, who are inclined to rebel against the authoritarianism they see, and hence incline to one extremism or another, developing a schism between themselves and their parents. Many young Jews have become political Leftists, only some of whom are supportive of Israel, while

*Some estimates are much higher.

others are sympathetic to the P.L.O. line.

There are, reportedly, several million Arabs in Latin-America. Many of these, originally Lebanese and Syrian, are Christian and not P.L.O. supporters. Nevertheless, Arab League propaganda is strong, and guerilla groups are said to receive much support from Libya and the P.L.O. The political Left, here as elsewhere, actively propagates the canard that Israel and international Zionism are "capitalist-imperialist-racist." Their governments have in general supported this position within the Third World and at the United Nations. This support, dominated by their oil and other economic interests is perhaps more rhetorical than it is real. Jewish leaders and organizations may compromise with the perceived necessity for this politique, and hence discount its domestic significance. But this creates a dilemma so far as many of their Jews, and especially their youth, are concerned. Anti-semitism meanwhile has been largely transmuted to anti-Zionism.

Given this set of circumstances, Jewish organizations are reluctant to approach official policy-makers with complaints. They are also inclined to distinguish carefully between specifically Jewish problems, and problems of broader application. They would prefer to take stands on human rights or international issues as individual citizens of their national communities, rather than as Jews, and wish that Jewish organizations outside their countries would also restrict themselves accordingly. Indeed, they have sometimes been embarrassed *visavis* their own goverments when Jewish organizations outside their countries have taken vigorous stands on questions not specifically Jewish.

While the Jews and Jewish communities of Latin America are not without serious problems, the greater uncertainties and dangers facing them do not arise primarily out of their Jewish identity. They arise in the first instance for those who, whether Jewish or not, take a principled stand against authoritarian governments, in the name of democratic principles and human rights, or who criticize openly the extremism practiced by either the Left and the Right. In the longer run, their security will depend on the resolution of this basic and pervasive struggle between Right and Left in Latin America.

Most of the people who live in these countries are poor. Given the nature of their governments, politics and class structure, the prospect of increasing radicalization and revolution from the Left cannot be ruled out. This is already happening in Central America. In such a case, well-to-do Jews would share the fate of the economic class of which they are a part. Yet if this tide is to be contained by ever more repressive governments, the present condition would become more aggravated. Only if Latin American governments succeed in finding increasingly progressive economic and political solutions to their problems can we expect the Jewish, as well as the human, condition in Latin America to improve in significant degree.

## Chapter Eight

# Other Selected Communities

To round out this review of Diaspora Jewry, we shall consider briefly the conditions of four selected and highly disparate Jewish communities — those of Iran, South Africa, Ethiopia and India. That of Iran is precarious; that of South Africa is perhaps best described as troubled; that of Ethiopia is literally life-endangered; and that of India is impoverished and almost completely isolated. The size, importance, history and problems of the first three all call for our attention. India is selected, arbitrarily, as one example of many small, isolated communities generally neglected and forgotten.

### *Iran*

In 1948, when the State of Israel was established, the ancient Jewish community of Iran, some 2,500 years old, numbered some 160,000. Approximately half of the community quickly responded to the opportunity to emigrate to Israel. Up to the revolution which ousted the Shah, the community's numbers remained at some 80,000. It has since been reduced to little more than half that number. The community had been one of mixed economic and social status. There were many very wealthy among them, and a quite sizable proprtion of well-to-do. But there were also very many poor and extremely poor. The poor presumably make up a large proportion of those remaining in Iran.

The new Islamic constitution of Iran accords religious freedom to Jews and other religious minorities. But the Khomeini regime distinguishes sharply between Jews and Zionists. The defense of or assistance to Zionism and Israel is considered treason and has already served to invoke capital punishment. Jews are considered moreover to have been friends or allies of the Shah's regime, and this makes their condition very precarious indeed, especially because severe restrictions have been imposed on emigration and travel abroad. It is reported that

Jews who wish to leave for a limited time must designate guarantors who will stand responsible for their return, or face severe penalties if they do not. Jews who wish to emigrate may do so, provided they leave practically all their possessions behind. Obviously, most of those who have left the country did so before these restictions were imposed. Of these, some 10,000 are said to have gone to Israel, with the majority going to the United States and Canada.

In an audience with the Ayatollah Khomeini in May, 1979, representatives of the Jewish community disavowed Israel and Zionism, and affirmed their dedication to the cause of the Islamic revolution. These protestations may shelter them for the time being. But internal tensions and unrest in Iran are great, and the internal situation is obviously explosive, quite apart from the external dangers which also threaten. The safety of Iran's Jewish community must therefore be regarded as extremely precarious.

## South Africa

The well-to-do, highly organized and strongly Zionist Jewish community of South Africa numbers some 120,000 Jews, who constitute a minority within the ruling white minority. The population has been maintained, despite a continuing emigration in recent years, by the influx of some 20,000 Israelis. More traditional in character than most Western Diaspora communities, the community has suffered correspondingly less from intermarriage, assimilation and demographic attrition. Thus, their birth rate is higher, and the proportion of elderly lower, than in the Western Diaspora communities. There is an excellent system of day schools, and fund-raising per head has been the highest of any Diaspora community. *Aliyah* to Israel has also been relatively high.

The chief problem of the South African Jewish community has been its difficulty in arriving at a consensus position with respect to the Government's *apartheid* policy. Many, perhaps most, Jews have been generally sympathetic to the aspirations of the blacks, who comprise an overwhelming majority of the country's population, and unhappy with the repression used to maintain the status quo. Nevertheless, there has been some diversity of opinion within the Jewish community, although not so much perhaps as among other sections of the populations, and many heart-searching debates on this question have taken place over the years. Until recently, this problem was resolved by mild resolutions recognizing the challenge, and leaving it to individual Jews to determine their own positions and conduct. This passivity troubled the conscience of many. It also caused great concern among those who felt that continuation of the *apartheid* policy would lead eventually to social explosion and tragedy. This concern indeed appears to have been responsible for much of the emigration experienced in recent years. In June 1980, finally, concerned about the slow pace of reforms and "the widening gulf and dangerous polarization" of race relations, the Jewish Congress unanimously adopted a resolution urging all concerned "to cooperate in securing the immediate amelioration and the ultimate removal of all unjust dicriminatory laws and practices based on race, creed or color."

Internal pressures by the underprivileged blacks have been complemented by external pressures by black African states and by the international community. But, the natural sympathies of Western democratic societies for the aspirations of South Africa's blacks and Western desires for cordial relations with African states have been tempered by their strategic interests. South Africa's mineral riches and her location governing the sea lanes around the Cape, especially for oil tankers too large to pass through the Suez Canal, cannot safely be ignored by Western countries dependent on their control by a friendly government. The situation is thus as awkward and delicate for the industrial democracies as it has been for the South African Jewish community.

One hopeful sign for improvement in this situation came in recent months from South Africa's new Prime Minister, who affirmed publicly that the Government must move progressively to deal with and ameliorate the racial question. Subsequent developments however have been less encouraging, and the future outlook remains uncertain.

## Ethiopia

The world was not aware, until sometime after the middle of the nineteenth century, that the Falashas of Ethiopia appeared to be Jews. The official recognition of the rabbinate of Israel that the Falashas were truly Jewish came only in very recent years. Currently, only some 28,000 survive of an ancient community which is said to have numbered 250,000 only a century ago.

The Falashas are concentrated in Gondar, a northern province of Ethiopia, where they live miserably in villages as sharecroppers and tenant farmers. Ethiopia's Marxist government seems well-disposed towards them. But plagued with secessionist war in both the south and north, its writ does not extend into the Gondar region, and the Falashas are powerless to resist punitive actions by the people amongst whom they dwell, or the raids by bandits and anti-government factions which kill or sometimes impress them into slavery. Neither can they benefit from the land reform measures the government has promulgated, but cannot enforce. The only bright light in their existence, and their only contact with the outside world, is that provided by the ORT, which has brought programs of agricultural improvement, schools, health care and Judaism to Falasha villages.

Only some 300 Falashas have thus far made their way to Israel. Although the desire of the entire community to make their way to Israel is reportedly very strong, diplomatic relations do not exist between Ethiopia and Israel, and emigration is not permitted. Interest in the Falashas' plight has finally been aroused, however, in both Israel and the Diaspora, and efforts are ongoing behind the scenes to effect their rescue. If these efforts fail, the prospects for the community's survival would appear to be very slim.

## *India*

The 7,500 Jews of India, concentrated almost entirely in the city of Bombay, constitute another ancient community which has managed to survive, despite its isolation, for 2,000 years.

A large proportion of the community are engaged in the lower and middle ranks of the civil service and, by Indian standards, are probably considered middle class. Most of them are nevertheless very poor, and few of their youth have the opportunity for education beyond the high school diploma. Their communal facilities are scanty and impoverished.

Indian Jews have no security problem. There is no anti-semitism or anti-Zionism, and emigration is open. Many thousands of them have gone on *aliyah* to Israel, assisted by a local Jewish Agency office. Despite reports that their emigres encounter discrimination in Israel with respect to jobs and housing, the emigration continues, and the community expects its numbers to decline by one-third by 1985. It has no rabbi, and the teachers in its two Jewish schools are unqualified. Intermarriage is not common.

Among the community's felt needs, the most important is the desire for scholarship assistance for its youth, since a university degree is still the high road towards upward mobility in India. It also desires a scholarly history to be done of the community, and is conscious of the need to salvage ritual and other religious items from village synagogues in the area around Bombay which are closing down.

# Part Three

# THE
# IMPLICATIONS
# OF PEACE

*Chapter Nine*

# The Implications of Peace for Israel

We stated at the outset of this report that we would concentrate our forward-looking effort on the implications and consequences of the Egypt-Israel peace over the near and medium term, and deal only very briefly and broadly wth the implications of a comprehensive peace. The road to peace, we also said, would be a long, arduous and unpredictable one. But because the future is not something which one day abruptly arrives, full blown in its own new image, but is rather shaped by the unfolding of events as the days pass into weeks, months and years, it is important to have a vision of what we desire the future to hold, so that we may attempt to give such direction as we can to its evolution. Though such efforts may be quite limited in their potential effect, our awareness of conscious aims will at the least improve our assessment of the trend of events. It is appropriate therefore to attempt first the more speculative longer term forward look.

## *Implications of a Comprehensive Peace*

In the framework of our report, a comprehensive peace is one which would be reached between Israel and her chief Arab adversaries. In the public discourse, at least until very recently, such a peace has generally been equated with "peace in the Middle East." This, in our judgment, reflects a serious confusion and error. Achieving comprehensive peace between Israel and her adversaries will be enormously difficult. But while such a peace might contribute to peace in the region, it could not possibly ensure it.

"The region's tensions," the New York Times sagely observed editorially some time ago, "are rooted in political, religious, national, dynastic and military rivalries *only marginally related to the Arab-Israel conflict . . .*" (our italics). One needs only to point to threatening tensions, rivalries and conflicts such as those between Iraq and Iran, Egypt and Libya, Iraq and Syria, Libya and Iraq, North and South Yemen,

[85]

and Algeria and Morocco, or to seething internal ethnic and religious differences within most of these countries where Shiites, Sunnis, Kurds and other groups are unreconciled to their societies and national governments, or to the struggle of antagonistic forces within Iran for control of the "revolutionary government," or to large immigrant working populations, many of them politically volatile Palestinians in the oil rich countries of the Persian Gulf, to become aware of the great internal instabilities and threats to peace throughout the region. But in addition to these dangers within the region, we must reckon with the external ones. It is here where the vital interests of the two great superpowers clash, where interests of East and West conflict, where the Western world is being sucked dry by OPEC, and where most of the Third World countries have vented their spleen against the industrial "capitalist-imperialist-racist" democracies by supporting, with little sense of discrimination, the Arab oil producers' and Palestinian causes.

If Israel-Arab peace does not then equate with peace in the region, and may not, if achieved, be followed by regional peace, an Israel-Arab peace might prove to be short-lived indeed, or in any event productive of only limited and unstable benefits. Much will depend, moreover, on the nature and terms of the peace, how and with whom it was negotiated, and how guaranteed. But because such scenarios take us straightaway into the completely unpredictable, we shall set aside provisionally these imponderable factors, and consider Arab-Israeli peace potentials as though they did not apply. But if it is useful, as we suggested earlier, to project a vision, it would be futile to attempt to delineate it in any detail. And it would be unrealistic to anticipate, after so long a period of mutual hostility, hatred and mistrust, that populations and their leaders on either side would be receptive and open to early cooperation to realize the potential benefits of peace. We would have to expect, rather, a longish period during which these divisions might be bridged by conscious, intelligent and patient efforts on both sides, and the benefits of peace would progressively be realized.

First and most obvious of the benefits of a genuine and reliable comprehensive peace, for Israel, would be a vast proportionate reduction in her military defense burden. The enormity of this burden is not easy to appreciate. Over the years, it has drained off as much as 30–35 percent of Israel's gross national product. A significant part of the defense burden, to be sure, has been provided, in some years, by external assistance which would presumably also be reduced as the defense burden declined. The burden of servicing the huge debt Israel has incurred would also remain. Only part of the reduction in defense expenditures would therefore become available to improve Israeli living standards or to increase investment for civilian purposes that would increase output and living standards later on. The benefits to the Israeli economy would nevertheless be very great. Many engaged in the military services would be released to the civilian economy. Facilities and resources used for military purposes would be freed for civilian production. Civilian living standards could rise, budget deficits could be reduced or eliminated, inflationary pressures would abate, balance of payments deficits could be reduced or possibly closed, and the social tensions aggravated by inflation and by a war and siege mentality would be eased. So would the intense internal political differences exacerbated by disparate views as to how outstanding issues with the Arabs and especially with the Palestinians should be resolved. Comparable benefits would of course also accrue to Israel's Arab adversaries, so far as Israel was concerned.

With comprehensive peace and the abatement of anti-Zionism, Israel's relations with the rest of the world could become normalized and more cordial. The door would be opened to regional cooperation, and to the expansion of trade relations and markets in Asia and Africa, as well as regionally. Israel's industry could achieve greater economies of scale, and become more competitive in international markets. Israel would become more attractive to foreign investment, and might well become a new center for international banking and finance, insurance and other services. Israeli science, technology and research capabilities in agriculture, health, education and other fields could contribute enormously to regional progress and welfare. Freed from day-to-day preoccupation with security considerations, her leadership could devote more time to rational social and economic policy-making and long term planning. In a condition of peace, Israel might succeed progressively in embodying, Jewish values into her society and way of life that could provide spiritual sustenance to Jews in the Diaspora.

All these, and much else, could be the beneficent consequences of a comprehensive peace. For reasons already stated, such prospects seem to lie beyond the foreseeable future. What we must now try to assess, more realistically, are the consequences and implications of Israel's peace with Egypt.

## Consequences and Implications of Partial Peace with Egypt

Peace with Egypt brought immediately to the fore two long-neglected, festering questions for Israel — one external, one internal — which demanded address. The first was the Palestinian question. The second was the inflation-ridden, tension-torn and critical condition of the Israeli society. Resolution of the Palestinian question was clearly an essential next step toward the building of a wider peace, and perhaps even toward the durability of the peace already concluded with Egypt. The state of Israel's economy, society and polity was, to be sure, a conequence of war and siege, and of mismanagement and

[87]

neglect, rather than of peace; but it was also a condition which, even in a state of only partial peace, could no longer be explained away, ignored or tolerated, and the improvement of which was essential to the realization of the potential benefits of the peace. Unfortunately, the immediate consequences of the peace with Egypt, and other developments, made Israel's recovery of economic and social health more difficult, rather than easier.

## The Palestinian Question

The negotiations with Egypt over autonomy for the West Bank and Gaza mandated by the Camp David accords focused attention on and sharpened long standing divisions within Israel as to how the problem of the West Bank — the core of the Palestinian question — should be resolved. Some Israelis favored annexation or indefinite retention of the area, either for security reasons or because they believed, on historical and religious grounds, that ancient Judea and Samaria should become part of Israel. Others opposed annexation or continued occupation. An Arab population multiplying at a much faster rate, they argued, would before long outnumber the Jewish population and change the fundamental character of Israel as a Jewish state. On the other hand, they maintained, if Arabs were not admitted to full citizenship or were held in subjection, this would subvert the democratic and humane character of the state. Some were prepared to negotiate with any Palestinian body that renounced terrorism and accepted peaceful negotiations as the only way to resolve the conflict. In return for recognition of Israel's right to exist as a Jewish state within secure and recognized borders, they were prepared to recognize the Palestinians' right to a national entity. But perhaps the largest single body of opinion was prepared to support the return of most of the West Bank to Jordanian sovereignty, or perhaps to an entity confederated with Jordan, provided strategic border adjustments were made for security purposes and the returned areas remained demilitarized.

Clearly, for most Israelis, an independent Palestinian state controlled by a terrorist P.L.O. still committed to Israel's destruction would represent an unacceptable threat. Since the kind of autonomy Egypt insisted upon would open the door to the creation of such a state, it was obvious Israel could not agree. Nevertheless, many Israelis resented the influence of extremist and non-security related views in shaping their own government's negotiating stance and especially its settlements policies, which suggested its intention to retain control of the entire West Bank indefinitely. This posture permitted the Arabs to focus the world's attention on Israel's role in endangering the peace-building process, and diverted attention from Arab rejectionism and Egypt's attempts to pre-determine a decision which, under the Camp David accords, was to be made only five years later.

The resulting failure to reach agreement on the autonomy has had serious consequences. It has increased tensions and conflict within Israel. It has made for increasing unrest and dissatisfaction among Israeli and West Bank Arabs. It has retarded the normalization of relations between Israel and Egypt. It has intensified the opposition of the Arab world to the Camp David accords. It has created strains in the Israel-U.S. relationship. It has lost for Israel much of the sympathy formerly displayed by West European countries who, while reconfirming Israel's right to live within secure, recognized and guaranteed borders, finally declared in June, 1980 that they were in favor of Palestinian self-determination, an end to Israel's territorial occupation and settlements, and P.L.O. "association" with the autonomy negotiations. It has confirmed, if not intensified, support for the Palestinian and Arab positions by the Third and communist worlds. And within the Diaspora, where most Jews seem to take a pragmatic view, and many have privately deplored what they considered the lack of realism and intransigence of the Israel government on these questions, it has added a new dimension of grave importance to already existing problems in the Israel-Diaspora relationship.

We identified earlier a number of problems which have developed over time in this relationship. But none of these, in the past, were related to the question of Israel's security. On this question, Diaspora Jews have been virtually unanimous in taking the view that, since it is the Israelis who must live with the consequences of such decisions or die in consequence of them, it is they who have the sole right to decide what their security requires. On West Bank issues currently, however, that unanimity is being severely tested, if not torn. If opinion on this question within Israel itself, including military opinion, is seriously divided, and if Israel's current policies seem to be heavily influenced by messianic as well as by security considerations, the pressures on Diaspora Jews to voice their dissent mount day by day, and have already begun to find expression, as Diaspora Jews began to perceive for the first time that support for Israel does not necessarily equate with support of its government's policies at any given time. The firm position taken recently, however, by the Government to permit only a strictly limited number of new settlements to be established in the future has moderated substantially the tensions previously aroused.

For a brief moment, after the revolution in Iran and the invasion of Afghanistan, it appeared possible that the U.S. and its Western allies might come to perceive in Israel a new strategic importance, and that this might modify their views of the importance or urgency of the Palestinian question. This was not the outcome. These events resulted initially in the attribution of greater strategic importnce to Egypt and to Saudi Arabia, rather than to Israel. It was the view of many observers that U.S. pressures on Israel to modify its policies sufficiently to reach agreement with Egypt would make themselves increasingly felt, once the presidential election in the U.S. was over. The war between Iraq and Iran however has now shattered the illusion that resolution of the Palestinian question would bring peace and stability to the Middle East and ensure the uninterrupted flow of oil supplies. This has made it both possible and necessary for the international community to view the Palestinian question in a broader and more realistic perspective. Because the views of the U.S. and its European allies, and ultimately public opinion in those countries, must inevitably play a major role in the resolution of the critical Palestinian question, we consider it timely to review at least briefly here the historical facts essential to an understanding of this most complex and difficult question.

Few Americans or Europeans know, for example, that until the Jewish people came to Palestine to establish settlements, the land they settled was largely barren, desolate and only sparsely populated, and Arabs came to settle there alongside the Jews chiefly because of the high wages and other benefits the settlements offered. Few of them know that the national homeland promised to the Jewish people by the Balfour Declaration in 1917 included the entire territory of the then Palestine, which included not only the West Bank but also Jordan; or that this Declaration was approved subsequently by the Governments of France and Italy, by the Supreme Council of Allied Powers, by the Council of the League of Nations and by the Congress of the United States. Few of them know that a number of Arab countries were granted independence at the same time, and by the same process, or that Emir Feisal of Iraq, at the Peace Conference in 1919, *welcomed* the creation of a Jewish national homeland. Few of them know that this Jewish national home, which then comprised over 43,000 sq. miles, was subsequently reduced in major degree by the separation of TransJordan (Jordan) in 1922 by unilateral action of the British Government, and by much more again when the State of Israel was created, only to be rejected by the Arabs. Within the Armistice lines which prevailed between 1949 and 1967, Israel's area comprised some 8,000 sq. miles, less than one-fifth of the original Palestine.

Few of them know that Israel's Proclamation of Independence guaranteed complete equality of social and political rights for all its citizens, including Arabs, without distinction of creed, race or sex, or that even as the new state was first attacked by her neighbors, Israel pleaded with her native Arabs to remain, and keep the peace, and play their part in the building of the State on the basis of full and equal citizenship; or that the Israeli Arabs who fled did so at the urging of the Arab governments attacking Israel, who subsequently denied their Arab refugee brothers a home, and imposed upon them the necessity to live in refugee camps. The clear aim of the Arab governments was to maintain a festering sore in existence, to be used as a continuing propaganda weapon against Israel, with a callous disregard of the needs and plight of these refugees whose cause they now ardently espouse.

Neither do most people now seem to recall that the 1967 borders to which the Arabs demand they return as a condition of peace are the very borders the Arabs violated when they forced Israel into war in 1967. Most importantly, very few seem to know or recall that during the 19 years from 1948 to 1967, when Israel was *not* in occupation of the West Bank, not one Arab country or statesman called for the creation of a second Arab Palestinian state there. (Jordan of course is a Palestinian state.) Neither do they seem to know that Jordan took possession of East Jerusalem by military force only in 1948, and that during the nineteen years of her occupation until Israel reclaimed it in 1967, the Jews were driven out and their holy places and cemetaries desecrated. Moreover, very few are aware of the very real degree of self rule which has prevailed in the West Bank under Israeli rule, or of the very substantial improvements in production and incomes which West Bank Arabs have been helped to achieve, or of the employment in Israel which has been afforded to many thousands of West Bank Arabs who commute daily to new well-paid jobs in Israel proper, or of the peaceful and cooperative co-existence which has characterized the relations between Jewish and Arab citizens of unified Jerusalem since 1967, until this was disrupted by P.L.O. formented terrorism against moderate Arabs as well as Jews.

Finally, we consider it necessary to remind men of good will that the 1967 borders to which it is demanded that Israel return would reduce her, at her vulnerable middle, to only nine miles in width, where her population centers would be vulnerable to even small artillery, and where she could be split in two by a tank advance within a matter of minutes; that a supposedly "intransigent" Israel has adhered scrupulously in the autonomy negotiations to the letter of the Camp David Accords; that it is Egypt that has been demanding concessions which go beyond the Accords, and that Egypt, as well as Israel, has sought to pre-determine outcomes which, under the Accords, are to be negotiated only five years after the autonomy agreement; that the alleged "illegality" of Jewish settlements in the West Bank, meanwhile, appears to be, at worst, a matter of interpretation and dispute, rather than a fact, no matter how impolitic or ill-timed some of the settlements may have been; and that Western impatience with what has seemed an interminable and unresultful negotiating process should be tempered by the recollection that, where vital matters of national security are involved, recent historical evidence — as in the years-long negotiations over Korea, Vietnam and the Panama Canal — attests to the time-consuming necessity of prolonged and deliberate negotiations, and the gradual evolution on both sides of a supportive public opinion necessary to the acceptance and durability of the agreements finally reached.

[91]

We do not recite this historical background in order to be tendentious with respect to the resolution of the Palestinian question, but rather because we consider it necessary to counter spurious propaganda which has been remarkably effective, and to help view the question in an informed and balanced perspective. Short memories, misunderstanding, impatience, short-sighted self-interest and sentimentality in the Western world could easily find expression in damaging pressures on Israel, rather than in constructive policies. In retrospect, it was naive to think at Camp David that resolution of the Palestinian question could be deferred until five years after the conclusion of an interim autonomy agreement. For it is clearly the basic differences over how that underlying question should be resolved which have made the desired interim autonomy agreement so difficult to achieve. That question is therefore effectively before us now. We believe these differences between Israel's security needs and Palestinian desires can be reconciled only if Palestinian representatives and the confrontationist Arab states agree:

1) to Israel's right to live at peace within recognized and secure borders;
2) to demilitarization of all returned territories, and to other essential security measures; and
3) to the normalization of diplomatic, trade and other relations with Israel.

Any interim autonomy agreement, to gain acceptance, would have to be compatible with, and conducive to, such an outcome. These requirements are in no way incompatible with the legitimate aspirations of the Palestinian people.

## Economic Burdens and Strains

A major immediate consequence of the partial peace with Egypt was, ironically, an enormous increase in the funds demanded by the military for defense purposes, the burden of which was already crushing. The return of the Sinai to Egypt, and the loss of the powerful and extremely costly network of defenses which had been put in place there over the years, required the construction of alternative defenses in the Negev within a relatively short period of time, at a cost of several billions of dollars. The return of the Sinai also involved the loss of the last of the important oil production facilities there, and heavy new foreign exchange expenditures to replace these vital supplies. It involved, further, costly indemnities and resettlement expenditures on behalf of the thousands of Israelis who had settled over a period of years in the strategically located Rafia salient near Gaza.

But the Negev defense redeployment and related Sinai costs were not the only factors contributing to pressures for added defense outlays. The rejection by the Arab states of the Camp David approach to peace, and their accelerated and threatening military build-up, could not be ignored. Saudi Arabia's huge purchases of the most highly sophisticated weaponry which, even if not used directly against Israel, might be made available for such use by others, was especially disturbing. Scarcely less so were comparable military build-ups by Iraq, Jordan, Libya and others; the abrupt change in Iran from a friendly regime to one marked by implacable hostility; the continued use of Southern Lebanon by the P.L.O. as a base for terrorist activities against Israel, and the ineffectiveness of the United Nations forces stationed there in controlling their activities; the continued and unconcealed support by the Soviet Union and Libya of terrorist organizations and activities; and the increasing engulfment of the Middle East and the Israel-Arab conflict in the wider East-West confrontation there. Indeed, the enhanced strategic role which the U.S. openly vested in Egypt and Saudi Arabia as significant allies in this growing confrontation, and its assistance in accelerating the rate and quality of their military build-ups, imposed the need for additional offsetting security measures on Israel.

Especially in the Israeli setting, the effects of these enlarged defense requirements could not be isolated, but impinged directly and heavily on the problems of inflation, the balance of payments deficit, long-starved housing and other social needs affecting largely new young families and poor Sephardic Jews, and many others. For some, the security outlook undoubtedly influenced their advocacy of a dynamic settlements policy on the West Bank, intensifying political divisions within Israel, and aggravating its external relations as well.

Early recognition of the potential inflationary impact of the Negev redeployment did lead to measure which would at least partially offset it. The U.S. provided for part of its financing in a combination of grants and loans and, to reduce strains on Israel's limited manpower and to curb inflationary spending in the domestic market, arranged to have the new airfields built with the use of foreign contractors, equipment and labor. In addition, taking a calculated security risk, the construction period of some projects was stretched out beyond the original three-year target date which had been geared to coincide with Israel's complete withdrawal from the Sinai. Despite such measures, however, defense demands on the budget inexorably increased, and became central to the fight against inflation belatedly undertaken late in 1979.

The fight against inflation was, essentially and at its core, a fight to effect very sizeable reductions in the government's huge deficit spending. Large-scale government subsidies used to reduce and contain the prices of many commonly used items and services were slashed. Government development programs and projects were frozen. Government loans for business investment and for housing mortgages, previously unlinked to the rate of inflation, were now fully or partially linked, thus ending or reducing their subsidization. Stringent cuts in the requested budgets of government departments were proposed, not only as economy measures, but also to reduce excessive staffing and to release manpower for transfer to more productive occupations. Stubborn efforts were also made to hold the line against wage and price increases throughout the economy.

These measures naturally evoked intense protest from the ministies, departments and the economic groups chiefly affected, each of them interested primarily in their own problems and seeking exemption from the general austerity which it was necessary for the society as a whole to share. Low and middle income groups felt keenly the sharp price increases in foods, fuels, transportation services, electricity and so on which followed the reduction or removal of subsidies. Newly formed families were confronted, not only by soaring prices for apartments, but also by sharply higher interest costs on mortgage loans. Many thousands of families living in pockets of urban poverty and in development towns, mostly of Sephardic origin and with large families, felt themselves especially ground down. Protest against West Bank settlements came not only from those who opposed continued occupation of the territories or who felt they were an obstacle to the peace-making process, but also from those who resented the large-scale expenditures the government was willing to make for these settlements in the face of serious housing shortages within Israel itself. Employers, exporters, workers, public servants all fought vigorously to protect their profit margins, incomes or jobs. But the sharpest fight of all was over the defense budget.

Israel's budgetary expenditures are divided about equally among three major expenditure categories — defense, debt service and social welfare. The huge external debt service burden must of course remain inviolable against cuts, if Israel's credit standing is to be protected, and her future borrowing needs are to be met. If defense requirements were to be protected, the concentration of required budget cuts on social welfare alone would be intolerable. The Finance Minister had no alternative therefore but to seek to impose substantial reductions in the requested defense budget. On this issue the Defense Minister chose to resign, briefly endangering the life of the government. The Prime Minister, assuming the Defense portfolio, sought to effect a compromise which would satisfy the demands of the Finance Minister for the minimum volume of budget cuts he considered essential, and the allocation of these among the Defense and other Ministries. Whether such compromise could be reached without seriously vitiating the fight against inflation, or without endangering the country's security, remained in question.

It was clear that the decades long practice of avoiding or postponing difficult economic choices and issues — of deferring painful costs by borrowing against the future — had run out of time. Israel had borrowed to the point where there was no longer a significant net margin left between the additional resources she could mobilize from abroad and the present costs of servicing her outstanding debts. Even with large borrowing, therefore, she could no longer consume much more than she could produce. The future had arrived, and it was clear that implementation of the painful measure necessary to deal with it would require a much greater determination, political courage and multi-party cooperation within the government than the present or previous governments had been able in the past to display. Yet an unswerving persistence in the fight against inflation, whether by the present or successor governments, was a *sine qua non* for Israel's return to economic and social health. This implied that in considering her security needs, Israel would have to rely in significant degree on the continued good will, assistance and assurances of the U.S. Government, to supplement her own military strength.

We trust therefore that the anti-inflation effort will continue. But we also recognize that the process will inescapably be painful. The measures necessary to curb inflation must demand sacrifices of one kind or another from all elements of the population. Unless people feel that these sacrifices are being fairly shared by all in rough proportion to their ability to carry the load, opposition is likely to be intense, and societal frictions will inevitably be exacerbated. For this reason, we believe it is of the outmost importance that all major groups in the society be involved in the ongoing formulation and supervision of the anti-inflation program, and that the program provide for special assistance to those whose living standards are or may fall below acceptable norms.

The outstanding early consequences of the peace with Egypt have thus been characterized by intense economic, social and political strains and conflicts. We turn from these now to consider other aspects and implications of the peace with Egypt.

## United States Aid

In all the world, Israel has one powerful friend and staunch supporter — the United States of America. U.S. political, military and financial aid have been, and remain, vital to Israel's security and survival. In a war of more than a few weeks' duration, Israel could not continue to protect herself in the absence of supplies from the U.S. In the absence of a U.S. veto in the U.N. Security Council, there is no knowing what sanctions might be imposed on Israel to enforce her compliance with imposed "solutions" to her differences with the Arab world. In the absence of continued sizeable financial aid, Israel's economy and living standards would go into a tailspin. In view of this obvious and very great dependency, what are the implications of the peace with Egypt, and the initial consequences of that peace we have just reviewed, for the reliable continuation of U.S. aid in the future?

The U.S. commitment and its aid to Israel are deeply rooted in U.S. national interestes and foreign policy. The U.S. has a major national interest in the survival and security of governments dedicated to democracy, free institutions and the dignity of man. Its interest in Israel, moreover, is multi-faceted. Israel is anti-Communist, a reliable friend in whose creation and subsequent well-being the U.S. played a major role, a country with close common cultural ties and religious roots. Americans have long admired the Israelis' pioneering spirit and accomplishments, their self-reliance, and their courage and skill in defending themselves, at great odds, against repeated aggressions. The natural sympathies and support of the respected American Jewish community have also been an important factor in the relationship.

U.S. national and security interests in the Middle East are not however confined to Israel alone. Stability and peace in the region, and the uninterrupted flow of oil supplies essential to the security and welfare of the U.S., Western Europe and Japan, are also major U.S. national security objectives. So, more broadly, is the maintenance of unity and harmony in the Western alliance. It cannot be expected, therefore, that U.S. aid to Israel will be unqualified in any and all circumstances. It must rather be expected that U.S. aid to Israel in the future, as indeed it has been in the past, will be tempered to the extent necessary to make it compatible with these other U.S. major national interests and concerns. Anticipations as to whether and how the U.S. may temper its aid to Israel to reconcile its several perceived national interests and objectives may vary both between and within the U.S. and Israel, and U.S. perceptions in this regard may also vary over time, with changing internal and external developments. The Iraq-Iran war, the most recent development, can only underscore the vital importance of Israel's survival and security to the U.S. and the entire democratic world.

In its efforts to promote Israel-Arab peace and general peace and stability in the region, the U.S. has placed great reliance on the Camp David approach to peace. It, and the democratic world, perceive agreement between Israel and Egypt on autonomy for the West Bank and Gaza as essential to the success of that approach. The U.S. has nevertheless refused to exert pressure on Israel to bridge its differences with Egypt in the autonomy negotiations, and concentrated its efforts on trying to bring the parties closer to agreement. This position is not likely to change. Recognition of this by President Sadat, together with his recent statement that he no longer recognized the P.L.O. as the sole legitimate representative of the Palestinians, could significantly improve the prospects for an agreement.

Although U.S. financial aid to Israel is not divorced from the political and military aid on which attention has just been centered, it does involve other considerations as well. While Isral's policies have placed increasing need and reliance on growing volumes of such assistance, political and economic developments in the U.S. have operated to make a continued positive response to such requests increasingly problematical. Israel and Egypt are currently beneficiaries of nearly three-quarters of all U.S. foreign aid. But in U.S. conditions of slow economic growth, inflation, unemployment and unsatisfied domestic needs, existing pressures for the curtailment of foreign aid in general are not likely to dissipate, and even the maintenance of aid to Israel (and Egypt) at current levels might well come under attack. Since current levels of U.S. aid to Israel provide little net aid after current debt service requirements, it would seem that the outlook for net financial aid in any significant amount is dour. Indeed, it cannot be excluded that debt service requirements, before long, will exceed new assistance levels, resulting in a deficit balance in these accounts.

## Economic Cooperation with Egypt

A number of early studies and analyses of the potentials for Israel-Egypt economic cooperation seem to agree on several fundamental points. They find, first, that these potentials are quite modest, rather than very considerable or great; that the most obvious early avenues of cooperation lie in tourism, trade and transportation; that the Egyptians are wary of an early and vigorous Israeli thrust to develop economic cooperation on a substantial scale; that Israeli approaches to such cooperation should therefore be careful, modest and low profile; and that prospects in the early stages would be improved if projects for economic cooperation were proposed in collaboration with third parties (U.S., European) so as to introduce a multilateral aspect to the cooperation process. Awareness of these and similar considerations appears to be widespread in both Israel and egypt. The likelihood is therefore that their approaches to the process will be careful and deliberate, thus improving the chances that fewer mistakes will be made and once begun, that a firm foundation will be laid for a constructive and growing cooperation in the future.

With this general background in mind, it is possible to point to basic economic factors which could support constructive economic cooperation between the two counties. Egypt has an abundant and relatively low cost labor supply, and relatively abundant energy and water. Israel is energy, labor and water short, but rich in technicians and a high state of technology in certain fields. Israeli technology, especially in the fields of agriculture and irrigation, desalination and solar energy, could contribute importantly to Egypt's current and future needs. Many Israelis, to be sure, believe that it would be unwise, for societal reasons, to open her borders to a sizeable influx of Egyptian workers. This is not to say however that Israeli entrepreneurs and possible third party partners might not set up industrial plants in Egypt to utilize the labor force available there. There are, analogously, reluctances to logical resource combinations on the Egyptian side. For example, the water short Sinai desert would be an obvious area for development with Israeli technical know-how and agricultural and water technology. Yet it seems unlikely, for psychological and political reasons, that Egypt would be ready to welcome cooperation in an area so long occupied by Israel, before some years had passed. Such considerations would not necessarily impede, however, the consideration of other major projects in fields like agriculture, food processing, construction, chemicals, textiles, tourism and others.

Such largely theoretical studies of economic cooperation possibilities as have been made cannot really uncover the many practical possibilities which only operating firms can recognize when they begin to look into such possibilities on the spot, in the light of their own operational needs. One early review by Koor, Histadruth's industrial conglomerate, for example, turned up a number of interesting practical possibilities which had not previously been recognized. These included the use of Israel oil extraction facilities for oil-seeds abundantly available in Egypt, for which extraction facilities were lacking; Israeli importation of industrial grade oranges from Egypt for the production and export of concentrates; the development of under-used Egyptian shrimp fisheries for Israel's established foreign markets; joint import of sponge iron in shipload quantities, too large for either Israel or Egypt to handle alone, at much lower cost; and so on. These are only illustrative of a potential multitude of analogous possibilities. The economic cooperation potentials of mutual benefit to both countries may therefore be much more considerable than has been realized. These of course can be identified and implemented only over time, as cooperation gets under way and develops.

Economic cooperation, for both countries, is part of the "normalization process" envisioned by their peace treaty. The indications are that Egypt has chosen to gear this important aspect of "normalization" to progress in the autonomy negotiations, despite her clear obligations under the peace treaty. Consequently, a meaningful start in the economic cooperation process may not be likely until basic ussues concerning the autonomy have been resolved.

As in the case of Israel, peace for Egypt has also meant grave economic, social and political problems in the early years, and large beneficial potentials in the longer run. Inflation, unemployment, large balance of payments deficits, a huge external debt service burden and her desire to modernize her military establishment are only part of the story. Egypt has serious food, nutritional and housing shortages. Health conditions are very poor. Transport, communications, electric power, water supply and other infrastructure facilities are badly run down and in need of major maintenance or replacement. In addition, Egypt is being boycotted by the Arab states and the economic aid formerly received from them has been terminated. Despite these difficulties, the Egyptian people appear to expect that peace will bring substantial gains in terms of improved living conditions, in the near future. This exposes them to the danger of dashed hopes and disillusionment which could threaten political stability and the peace-building process. Clearly, therefore, Egypt as well as Israel will need massive economic investment and aid in the years immediately ahead. The stakes of the U.S. and Western Europe in this matter are obviously great. The costs of building peace may be very large; but the costs of failure would be infinitely greater. The possible contributions of a Middle East Development Corporation for the private sector and joint projects of both countries, and of a Middle East Development Bank or Fund, both internationally financed, should therefore be actively explored.

## Foreign Direct Investment

Peace with Egypt has done little to affect the external and internal factors which have kept foreign direct investment in Israel at disappointing low levels for many years.

Among the external factors, we need to note only the drag of high oil prices on worldwide economic activity and growth; the pervasive effects of the Arab boycott; the intensified balance of payments and other pressures on most non-oil producing countries to maximize their exports and reduce their imports; and the turmoil, and the ever latent threat of renewed or widened hostilities, in the Middle East. The even more important internal negative factors have been mounting inflation and continuous currency devaluation; limitations on the availability of manpower for industrial occupations; the low utilization of productive capacity; unsatisfactory levels of worker productivity; a preponderance of small, family-owned and inefficient traditional industries oriented primarily to the small domestic market with little interest in either exports or foreign partners; and an image of Israel which presents many discouraging aspects to prospective foreign investors. This image is a compound of prevailing impressions concerning Israel's excessive and burdensome government controls, the dominant role and excessive power of the trade unions, the large number of unsuccessful ventures in the past, the inadequacy of telephone and other public services, favoritism to Histadruth and other socially-owned enterprises in the awarding of government contracts, an unnecessary, time-consuming, costly and frequently vexatious volume of red-tape in dealing with the government bureaucracy, and a mistrust of private business in general.

In marked contrast to these negative elements which contribute so heavily to Israel's investment climate are a number of positive elements which are potent both individually and cumulatively. Over the last decade or so, Israel has developed a booming export sector based on a number of outstanding "success stories" in high technology, science-based and innovative (including fashion) industries which are well-managed, efficient and internationally competitive. These impressive export successes rest on Israel's most significant comparative advantage for prospective foreign investors — the availability in Israel of a wealth of highly trained scientist, engineers and technicians of all kinds, backed up by outstanding reasearch centers and institutions with tremendous applied research capabilities, all available at salaries and other costs far below those prevailing in the U.S., Western Europe and Japan. This significant advantage is especially attractive to science-based, high technology industries which must devote a substantial part of their sales revenues to research and development for new and improved processes and products.

Another significant potential advantage Israel can offer lies in the duty free access she enjoys in entering the Common Market and the U.S. market for a wide variety of products. This should make investment and manufacture in Israel more attractive to U.S. producers for export to the Common Market, and for Common Market producers interested in exporting to the U.S.

Finally, note should be taken of the very substantial incentives Israel offers to foreign investors, which in some cases may make the costs of attracting the new investment dollar more costly to the Israel economy than the benefits gained.

If, on balance, the foregoing analysis portrays a rather mixed picture with a tilt to the unfavorable side, this confirms and helps broadly to explain Israel's disappointing foreign direct investment experience in the past. But does it also explain why wealthy Jewish business men, given their special motivations and Israel's needs, may not be expected to invest much more actively in Israel than they have in the past? The simplest answer is to observe that, for most business men, philanthropy and business do not mix. Giving is easy. It demands only parting with money. Investment, to be successful, demands the input of time and personal involvement, and a combination of factors — an investment climate — conducive to success. These are not very different for domestic or foreign investors, or for Jewish or non-Jewish investors. The measures needed to make foreign direct investment in Israel much more attractive are the same measures, basically, that are needed to restore Israel to economic and social health.

## Jewish Migration – Aliyah and Yerida

Peace with Egypt has probably lessened the security concerns of many Jews contemplating emigration to Israel. This may well have been offset however by knowledge of the great economic difficulties Israel is currently experiencing. Jewish migratory movements are likely to be most influenced by difficulties in the lands where they are now residing, and their assessment of the relative attractions and opportunities in lands open to their immigration, rather than by the peace with Egypt.

We have already discussed at some length the problems and issues of Soviet Jewry, and their current and prospective migration. Here, we shall only repeat that the number of Jews the Soviet Union will permit to depart promises to remain a matter of great uncertainty, and that the question of what efforts, if any, the Jewish organizations of the U.S. and other Diaspora communities can and should make to persuade a larger proportion of them to emigrate to Israel, remains to be resolved.

The coming months or years could see a considerable emigration of Jews from other lands. Untoward and sudden developments in Iran — of which there have already been dangerous harbingers — could send most of her 40,000-50,000 remaining Jews streaming our of the country, perhaps mostly to Israel. Deterioration of racial relations and intensified outbreaks of racial violence in South Africa might lead to a substantial rise in Jewish emigration from that country, although Israel might not be the destination for as large a proportion as in the case of Iranian Jewry. Ways might be found to enable a substantial number of Falashas to leave Ethiopia for Israel. Political development in Latin American countries might increase Jewish emigration considerably, wtih many going to Israel. It is difficult however to foresee much of an increase over the relatively low levels of Jewish emigration from the U.S. and Western countries to Israel, despite Israel's intense desire for *aliyah* from those countries.

The prospective movements of Israelis from or back to Israel are perhaps somewhat less problematical. Most of the estimated 350,000-500,000 *yordim* now living abroad, chiefly in the U.S., left Israel primarily in search of greater opportunities, income and comforts than were available to them at home. These they have presumably found and would find it extremely difficult to leave. Moreover, any lingering sense of guilt they may have retained for having left their families and friends to face hazards they were unwilling to share would have been at least somewhat relieved by the peace with Egypt. On the other side of the coin, it would appear that many Israelis who previously resisted the temptations to leave Israel, because they were unwilling to appear to desert their country in a time of danger, may no longer feel this constraint in the same degree. The pull of opportunity and of friends and family already abroad, and the push of inflation, economic slowdown, housing shortages and austerity at home may well increase substantially the volume of emigration from Israel in the coming period.

In this regard, as well as in many others, we recognize the very great importance of Israel's restoration to economic and social health.

*Chapter Ten*

# The Implications of Peace for Diaspora and for Israel-Diaspora Relations

In addressing the implications of peace for Israel, we chose to assess first the implications of a comprehensive peace. In doing so, we made no attempt to take into account such imponderable factors as the distinction between an Israel-Arab peace and peace in the Middle East, or the nature and terms of the peace, or how and with whom it might be negotiated, or how long it might take to bridge old animosities and suspicions. We then turned, more realistically, to a consideration of the consequences and implications of the peace with Egypt. We shall follow the same procedure here. Part of the discussion will involved consideration of some of the same phenomena, but from a different point of view.

For more than thirty years, concern for Israel's security and survival, and efforts to assure them, have been the chief motivation for the organized efforts of most Diaspora Jews, and the chief expression of their sense of Jewish identity. To the extent that a comprehensive peace between Israel and her Arab adversaries reduced these dangers, and Israel's remaining insecurities increasingly resembled those faced by the Western world as a whole, rather than being particular to Israel, it would seem that the effects on Diaspora Jewry would almost of necessity be profound.

These effects, to be sure, would not come all at once, or even within the span of a few short years. For one thing, it would take some time before confidence in the reliability and durability of such a peace could begin to grow. Further, Diaspora Jews would surely remain deeply concerned with Israel's efforts to achieve economic and social health. And, as long as there existed harassed or endangered Diaspora communities which might need to flee to Israel as a haven, other Diaspora Jews would without question remain involved. Nevertheless, a relatively secure Israel, or an Israel sharing a far more general insecurity, could scarcely be expected to evoke the same kind of intensity of response and commitment that has been characteristic of Diaspora Jewry for the past three decades. Most Diaspora Jews would increasingly need to find new stimuli to maintain their sense of Jewish identity, or that sense would tend to weaken.

It may be expected, moreover, that the conjuncture of world trends which increasingly threatens the industrial democracies will cause Jews in those societies to focus more attention on the threat to the security of their native lands and to the democratic values they cherish. These broader concerns, to be sure, do not conflict with or challenge a sense of Jewish identity or commitment to Israel. Their effect rather may be to blend or diffuse these within a more comprehensive perspective. The net effect of such a change might however be no less real or significant.

This new element, it will be noted, is one which would be superimposed on others long existant and earlier discussed — generational leadership and change, acculturation, intermarriage, secularization and assimilation. The question we are considering here calls upon us, logically, to anticipate the prospective effects of a comprehensive peace some two, three or more decades from now — on a *next* generation comprised of the sons and daughters of today — a generation more secular, more professional and more universalist, without direct memory of the Holocaust and with at most faint memories of the creation of the State of Israel and of its wars for survival. We do not need to attempt this logical exercise. The prospective reactions of this next generation are already inherent and discernable in many of their fathers and mothers today.

For that preponderant part of Diaspora Jewry whose attachment has been to Israel, rather than to Judaism and Jewish ways of life as such, it seems quite clear that a comprehensive peace, given present trends, must be expected progressively to result in a weakening sense of Jewish identity, a lesser concern for Israel and for other Jews, and in less identification with Jewish organizations and communal affairs. For that lesser body of Diaspora Jews who have retained a genuine attachment to Judaism, who have not needed to use fund-raising and other help to Israel as a surrogate for their religion and a crutch for their sense of Jewish identity, other effects may be anticipated. To such Diaspora Jews, a comprehensive peace might bring a renewed and re-invigorated need to enrich their Jewish way of life, and to find new expressions for their sense of Jewish identity. We may find such Jews giving much greater emphasis to Jewish religion, education and culture, in their own lives and in those of their children. For both these groups, however, much will depend on whether Israel continues along a basically materialist path, or whether she succeeds, in an era of peace, in building increasingly into her way of life the values and spiritual goals of Judaism. A materialist-minded Israel might well witness the progressive loss of modern secular Jewry in the Diaspora, and the turning away and growing inwardness of traditional Diaspora Jewry. An Israel which took the more ethical path might well contribute to the survival of the sense of kinship and peoplehood among secular Jews, and to enriching the Judaism of the others, as it enveloped them in an ever warmer embrace.

Israel's isolation in the international community has been accompanied, as we have noted, by a virulent anti-Zionism which identified Israel with neo-colonialism, racism, imperialism and capitalist exploitation. This anti-Zionism gave rise to or intensified a new anti-semitism in many countries of the Diaspora. With comprehensive peace and an ending of Israel's isolation, anti-Zionism should also abate, and with it, the anti-semitism it has aroused. This should be accompanied by a gradual easing of the renewed tensions and concerns which have afflicted many Jewish communities of the Diaspora.

These broad perspectives, and other implications of a comprehensive peace, lie at some indeterminate distance in the future. Our primary concerns must be with the presently recognizable consequences and the foreseeable implications of Israel's peace with Egypt.

## Consequences and Implications of the Peace with Egypt

By the time peace with Egypt arrived in March, 1979, the euphoria evoked by President Sadat's visit to Jerusalem in November, 1977, and that which still survived at the time of the Camp David accords, had largely evaporated. What remained was a sober awareness of how long, arduous and uncertain the road to a comprehensive peace would be. Rejection of the peace with Egypt by the Arab states had already been indicated. But Saudi Arabia's decision to join the rejection front, and to participate in the economic and political boycott declared against Egypt, was a disappointing surprise. Also disappointing was the persisting refusal of Jordan and West Bank Arabs to join the autonomy negotiations, and "moderate" Saudi Arabia's refusal to play a constructive role in that regard. The Saudi's termination of economic aid to Egypt also made the peace-making process more difficult and costly for President Sadat. These reactions and the isolation of Egypt in the Arab world placed great pressure on President Sadat to take a hard line in the autonomy negotiations.

The Diaspora's increasingly somber mood over these events has been accompanied by a growing unease and concern over the course of the autonomy negotiations seeking an interim resolution of the Palestinian question. As long as Israel's stand on this question was perceived to be based squarely on security considerations, support within the Diaspora was solid. There has been and is no doubt in the minds of Diaspora Jews about the need for secure and recognized borders, or the unacceptability of an independent Palestinian state on the West Bank and in Gaza dominated by the P.L.O., or the inviolability of a unified Jerusalem. But the increasing evidence provided by Israel's settlements policies, the manner of their implementation and the internal debate and dissent in Israel about them, that Israel's objectives were not based solely, or perhaps even primarily, on security considerations, created great difficulties of conscience for many Diaspora Jews. The government of Israel, they felt, expected them fully and unquestioningly to accept and support policies heavily influenced by a minority of extremists with little regard for U.S., world or Diaspora opinion and perhaps for the majority of Israeli opinion as well, irrespective of how they felt about them. Some troubled Diaspora leaders chose to remain silent. Others expressed their concerns in private meetings with Israeli officials, and endeavored to conceal their misgivings while supporting Israel's policies in dealings with their own governments. But some, defying a long-standing taboo, began openly to express their concerns, doubts or dissents. Such public expressions have been deplored by Government leaders in Israel, as well as by some Diaspora Jews. The former generally plead for a show of unity that will not lend aid and comfort to Israel's enemies. The Diaspora Jews who condemn such expressions add another argument. Diaspora Jews, they maintain, have no right to differ with Israel where her security policies are concerned, because it is the Israelis, and not they, who will have to suffer the consequences if peace efforts fail and hostilities are resumed.

This important and controversial issue requires examination here. As we see it, those who would uphold the taboo greatly oversimplify the case. First, Diaspora silence would neither mollify nor silence Israel's enemies; they would merely find or invent other means of attack. Second, important issues other than security are also involved in the policies in question. If these are indeed aimed at the continued occupation or annexation of the West Bank, they raise the questions of whether Israel is to become a binational state, or what the moral qualities of a Jewish occupying state would be. These questions are of great importance to all Jews, everywhere. Third, it is far from clear that the settlements and related policy objectives of the present government do or will in fact serve to promote Israel's security. Many Israelis, including military officers, assert the contrary. They claim rather that these policies will progressively radicalize and provoke West Bank Arabs into open defiance; that they will slow down and endanger the peace-making process; that their huge costs will further weaken Israel's economy and reduce its ability to support an effective fighting force; and that an Israel divided and embittered by differences over these policies will inevitably result in the lowered morale of the armed forces. Fourth, it is plain that Israel's security does not rest solely on her own military strength, borders, settlements, and ability to control the West Bank population. Her security rests heavily also on the good will and support of the Western democracies, chiefly the United States. In the U.S., Jewish leaders are better qualified to gauge the state and trends in official and public opinion on Israel's policies, and to assess their own ability to influence such opinion in favor of Israel. They cannot support these policies wholeheartedly unless they themselves find the policies credible and support-worthy. Lacking such conviction, they would themselves lose credibility if they attempt nevertheless to support them.

We believe that this issue is by far the most important of the many outstanding current issues between Israel and the Diaspora, and that independent Diaspora judgements require full expression in an uninhibited dialogue of the grave doubts and concerns occasioned by Israel's positions and policies.

These initial consequences of peace with Egypt coincided with, and were complicated and aggravated by, a number of other factors. Chief among these were the accumulating and ever more widespread awareness and concern in the Diaspora of grave social, economic and political weaknesses within Israel, and a corresponding awareness and concern with a number of other serious deficiencies in the Israel-Diaspora relationship which had accumulated over the years, which we discussed in an earlier section of this report. Intermixed with these was the disturbing recognition that Israel had failed in one major aspect of its twofold significance or mission for the Jewish people. It had created an independent State whose doors would always open and provide haven to Jews from anywhere in the world who needed it. But in the opinion of many, it had been unable — at least thus far — to create a Jewish State which would exemplify, for the Jews of the world and for the nations, the unique values and way of life which Judaism offered to the world.

One final point should perhaps be made. For the first time since the founding of the State, fund raising and loans to Israel could no longer serve as a major contribution by Diaspora Jewry to the solution of Israel's needs. Through 1972, contributions from Jewish sources, whether through institutional fund-raising or individual transfers, together with purchase of Israel bonds, amounted to more than half of all the external capital available to Israel. While the total of funds available from these Jewish sources increased very sizeably thereafter, they could not keep pace with Israel's exploding external capital needs. The U.S. Government became the largest single source of external funds, with Jewish sources dropping to only one-third of a much larger total that was still inadequate to Israel's requirements. But this was only part of the story. External capital was essential to Israel's balance of payments problem. But it could do little or nothing to help Israel to make peace, or improve the condition of poor Oriental or Sephardi Jews, or improve relations with Israel's large Arab minority, or eliminate serious differences between Orthodox and other Jews, or relax mounting tensions and conflicts among the political parties and social groups in a society rapidly becoming embittered and ungovernable. Neither could it do much to make inflation more manageable, or solve the housing problem. As more and more Diaspora Jews became aware of this new situation, their links to Israel, so heavily dependent on money-raising and giving, would become increasingly frayed. Their dependence on this link for their sense of Jewish identity would require a new structural link to be forged through which they could help to meet those other needs their money could not serve.

Peace with Egypt, then, has helped to crystallize feelings within the Diaspora that the time has come to address these basic questions which confront world Jewry. What is a just, a Jewish way, to peace? How can Israel restore herself to economic, social and political health, and how can the Diaspora best be of assistance in this major effort? How can Israel build the values and ideals of Judaism into her way of life? What is the proper relationship between Israel and the Diaspora? How can the Jewish communities of the Diaspora enter into a constructive and symmetrical dialogue with the sovereign state of Israel to resolve the difficulties which have evolved in their relationship, and to collaborate constructively in the building of a secure, meaningful and *viable* Jewish future? What institutional structure, framework or device could adequately represent and speak for the Diaspora in such a dialogue? Could the horizon of Jewish concerns be limited to issues that affected Jews only, or did that horizon have to be expanded to include the security, welfare and concerns of all those who subscribed to principles of human integrity, dignity and freedom wherever the democratic heritage is eroding and threatened?

# Summary Conclusions and Recommendations

## On Peace

Israel's peace with Egypt represents an indispensable and historic first step of the greatest importance on the road to Israel-Arab peace. That road however will be a long, arduous and dangerous one. Significant progress needs to be made towards that goal, so that the full potential of this historic opportunity may be realized, and that the peace with Egypt itself may be fruitful and enduring. *At this time, the essential next step along the road to peace is an agreement on the Autonomy or an alternative formula which will be both consistent with Israel's security needs and acceptable to the Arabs most directly concerned.*

A number of factors are responsible for, or have contributed to, the lack of progress in the autonomy negotiations thus far. The most important of these has been the refusal of the Arab world to accept the Camp David approach to peace, or the desirability of peace with Israel and its right to live within secure and recognized borders. It is these positions, held most fanatically by the P.L.O. and countries like Libya, Iraq, Syria and Algeria, which have kept Jordan and West Bank and Gaza Palestinian representatives from joining the autonomy negotiations, and prevented more "moderate" Arab countries like Saudi Arabia from playing a constructive role. Arab rejectionism has also had important effects on the negotiating stance and policies of both Egypt and Israel. Lacking the right to make commitments for either Jordan or the Palestinians of the West Bank and Gaza, and concerned about Egypt's relations with the rest of the Arab world, President Sadat seems to have felt obliged to take and maintain a hard line in the negotiations. He has demanded that Israel make concessions — notably on the settlements and on East Jerusalem — beyond those called for by the Camp David accords. He has also demanded full legislative powers for the "self-governing authority" whose powers and responsibilities were to be negotiated and which was also described in the accords as an "administrative council." On these, Israel, for whom — unlike the

Arabs — a miscalculation on security could mean literally liquidation and death, has been unyielding. Clearly, both Egypt and Israel have sought to ensure that the transitional authority agreed upon would lead to a resolution of the Palestinian question, five years later, that would be acceptable to themselves. But unlike Egypt, Israel has adhered strictly to the letter of the Camp David accords.

Short memories, misperceptions, impatience, sentimentality and short-sighted self-interest among West European countries have also contributed importantly to the lack of progress. Most recently, they have had the effect of encouraging Arab rejectionism and extremism, especially that of the P.L.O., and have thus weakened the Camp David approach to peace. These governments have been skillfully exploited by Arab propaganda and oil-powered political pressures, to which opinion in the United States has not been entirely immune. And because Israel's settlement policies on the West Bank were perceived to be motivated significantly by messianic considerations, with an eye to indefinitely prolonged occupation or annexation of the West Bank, rather than by security considerations alone, these policies have permitted the world's attention to be focused by the Arabs on Israel's alleged role in delaying progress on the autonomy by denying to Palestinian Arabs the realization of their legitimate rights. This has diverted attention from the far more basic factors responsible for the delays in the peace-making process.

This situation, most recently reflected in the extremely one-sided resolutions adopted last July and August by the U.N. General Assembly and Security Council, has now become critical. To retain and strengthen the support of the United States, and to regain the sympathetic understanding and support of Western Europe, both of which are indispensable, *it is vital that Israel's negotiating posture and policies be perceived to rest squarely and unequivocally on security considerations. Israel cannot safely permit the all-important peace and security objectives to be obstructed, distorted or manipulated, as in the case of some of the West Bank settlements, by the political leverage of small, ideologically extremist groups.* Mr. Begin's recent announcement that the number of additional settlements on the West Bank would be strictly limited has made an important contribution to this objective.

Our examination (in Chapter Nine) of the historical background of the Palestinian question does not address two current confusions relevant to the present impasse. *First*, while Israel's settlements policies, or the manner of their implementation, have suggested an intention on the part of the Begin government to extend indefinitely its rule, or to establish sovereignty, over the West Bank (Judea and Samaria), it should be clear that there is no necessary connection between settlements and sovereignty. While Israel would undoubtedly insist, for historic and religious as well as security reasons, that certain Jewish settlements continue on the West Bank under any agreement which might be reached, it does not necessarily follow that she would assert the right of sovereignty as well. *Second*, recognition in the Camp David Accords of the legitimate right of the Palestinian people to participate, through their elected representatives, with Egypt, Israel and Jordan in the determination of their own future, is not the same as "self-determination." Neither would the exercise of "self-determination," if conceded, necessarily call for the creation of an independent political entity. Two states — Israel and Jordan — already exist within the original Palestine Mandate. The majority of Jordan's population are Palestinians. There thus already exists one independent Arab Palestinian State. To argue the desirability of such a state does not require the creation of a *second* one. And it is by no means clear that, but for fears of P.L.O. terrorist reprisals and assassinations, either King Hussein of Jordan or Arab moderates in the West Bank and Gaza would opt, when the time came, for a second Arab Palestinian entity. The West European governments who declared at Venice that the P.L.O. should be "associated" with the autonomy negotiations would have been well advised to take into account the possibility that West Bank and Gaza Palestinians, given a free choice, might prefer an autonomy in confederation with Jordan, or some other solution, rather than a P.L.O. led entity which might lead them to war with Israel, or Jordan, or both.

Peace in the Middle East however does not depend on resolution of the Israel-Arab conflict alone. Increasing regional and international tensions — Soviet moves in the Horn of Africa and Afghanistan, OPEC price aggression and supply threats, chaos in Iran, dangerous instabilities and hostilities within and among the Arab states, the Soviet-Arab-Third World coalition against the free democratic societies — all these and, more recently, the Iraqi-Iranian War, make it clear that resolution of the Palestinian question and Israel-Arab peace, even if achieved, will not ensure peace in the Middle East. The turbulence within, and the hostilities among, Arab states "are rooted in political, religious, national, dynastic and military rivalries only marginally related to the Arab-Israel conflict." These are compounded by the East-West and North-South confrontations and by conflicting interests over control or assured access to vital oil supplies, all of which cross paths in the Middle East. The Soviet Union's military incursion into Afghanistan, following on her earlier power moves in the Horn of Africa and elsewhere, and now the Iran-Iraq War, have heightened these dangers enormously. It may well be therefore that substantial progress towards Israel-Arab peace cannot be attained until some of these larger dangers are reduced or resolved. It is, clearly, not only Israel's security, but the security and well-being of the Western world, which are at hazard in the Middle East.

In view of the foregoing, *we further recommend and urge:*

a) that the Government of Israel make unmistakeably clear, in its statements, policies, negotiations and actions that its search for peace is based squarely and unequivocally on security considerations;

b) that the Government of Israel, in close cooperation with Diaspora communities, mount urgently a massive educational campaign in the United States and key countries of Western Europe to inform their citizenries of the facts essential to an understanding of the Palestinian question, and of other dangerous instabilities in the Middle East, so that they can assess the problems of Israel-Arab peace-making in a balanced and informed perspective;

c) that the Government of Egypt correct and refrain from any further actions inimical to the peace-making process (e.g., its obstruction of the process of economic and cultural normalization, its efforts to dissuade African nations from re-establishing relations with Israel, its premature invocation of the issue of East Jerusalem in disregard of an earlier understanding, and its vote in favor of the July, 1980 General Assembly Resolution which subverted Security Council Resolutions 242 and 338 on which the Camp David Accords were based); that it collaborate in good faith to bring the autonomy negotiations to a timely and successful conclusion; that it honor fully its obligations under the Peace Treaty to cooperate in the expeditious and concrete realization of the normalization of relations process with Israel; and further, that the Government of the United States use its good offices to persuade Egypt accordingly;

d) that Western governments give their full support to the Camp David approach to peace, and refrain from exerting pressures on Israel to accede to demands which would gravely endanger her security;

e) that Western governments recognize that it is vitally necessary that they display the determination to take whatever concerted action may be necessary to assure the required degree of political stability in the Middle East and a reliable flow of essential oil supplies at tolerable prices;

f) that Western governments seek also to relieve the crushing burden of intolerable oil prices on the non-oil producing developing countries, and the dangers which financing the resulting foreign exchange deficits pose for the already-overburdened international banking and financial system, by advocating that OPEC provide oil to these countries at prices they can afford, and by insisting that the oil-rich surplus countries accept responsibility for financing poor countries' oil-induced foreign exchange deficits directly, rather than through the recycling process;

g) that the Diaspora communities in the democratic societies recognize that the security, well-being, civilization and values of the democratic world are in danger, and that they broaden their activities to sharpen Western perceptions of these dangers, and to strengthen their mutual resolve to address and repel them.

Israel faces three major and priority tasks at this time: 1) to build a secure peace; 2) to put her internal house in order; and 3) to develop a healthier and more constructive relationship with the Diaspora. As she moves to fulfill these, a fourth major and priority goal lies immediately beyond — namely, progressively to embody in her way of life the values and spiritual goals which Judaism brought forth and contributed to the world.

The advent of peace with Egypt found Israel beset with a number of economic, social, religious and political problems so grave and basic in their nature as to constitute an internal danger to the future of the State second in magnitude only to the external danger she has repelled at great cost for the past three decades. Moreover, for a number of reasons, including the very large costs involved in the redeployment of Israel's defenses from the Sinai to the Negev, the surrender of Sinai oil and the absorption of higher levels of immigration by Soviet Jews, Israel's economic burdens during the early period of peace with Egypt have been aggravated, rather than relieved.

Very high inflation, a huge balance of payments gap, a debilitating internal and external debt burden, serious imbalances in the structure of production and employment and too low productivity are Israel's chief economic problems. Strained relationships between Western (Ashkenazi) and North African and Asian (Oriental or Sephardi) Jews; between Israel's Jewish population and her Arab minority; among the highly orthodox, Jews of other denominations and secular Jews; intolerable housing shortages and costs; intensely factional and highly unstable politics; confusion and dissent over the government's West Bank (Judea and Samaria) and settlement policies; the disruption of behavioral norms evident in group and inter-personal relations which have become increasingly selfish and even violent or criminal — all these, superimposed on economic disorder, have seriously weakened the social fabric of the nation. Similar or analagous problems, to be sure, may be observed in most industrial societies. What makes Israel unique in these respects are her external dangers, the degree and intensity of these internal problems, her lesser material resources for dealing with them and chiefly of course, our concerns for her well-being.

Most of these conditions are not new. Although they have grown swiftly in recent years, their origins go back in some cases to the early days of the State. Several reasons underlie the failure of successive governments to deal with them effectively. A lack of basic economic grasp, ideological illusions, the strains of industrialization and urbanization, preoccupation with war and siege and still other factors, including disregard for the advice of the government's economic planners, have all been responsible for growing income disparities, excessive dependence on external resources and other manifestations of the social and economic malaise which Israel faces. But also responsible in a very important degree has been a flawed electoral system based on proportional representation. This has produced a multi-party political system and successive coalition governments which could make no important decisions without the consent of their numerous and contentious party constituents (some very small), and which were hence incapable of resolving basic issues. In consequence, such issues over the years have been compromised, or postponed, or evaded, or distorted — but they have not been solved. What Israel faces today is an accumulation of exacerbated and festering issues of grave proportions.

Late in 1979, the Government of Israel designated a new Finance Minister and declared its approval and support of his determination to mount and carry through a vigorous anti-inflation program. This program included severe budget cuts, a freeze on hiring in government employment, a tough line on wage increases, strict curbs on government investment projects, the termination of unlinked government loans to business and for housing and the phased elimination of price subsidies. The program naturally encountered a great deal of resistance. A year later, its results were at best disappointing. Its bitterly contested efforts had brought about a slowdown in economic activity, a rise in unemployment and a decline in real personal incomes and consumption. The balance of payments gap had been somewhat reduced in spite of a large rise in the cost of imported oil. But the battle of the budget — the core of the anti-inflation effort — was still raging, and the rate of inflation was higher, not lower, than it had been before.

We consider it to be of the utmost importance and urgency, and *we recommend that the government of Israel, despite the pressing claims of external problems, pursue its anti-inflation policy with unwavering persistence.* Fortunately, because inflation is so closely interrelated with many other problems, significant progress on this front will automatically ease pressures on many others, and make it less difficult to deal with them. *We stress again however that success in curbing and reducing inflation in significant measure requires the understanding and active collaboration of the major economic groups within the society, and especially that of workers and employers. Such understanding and collaboration can only be achieved and maintained over time if the representatives of such groups are made full and active partners in what must be a truly national effort.*

Although fiscal and monetary policies and measures are obvious first steps in fighting inflation, and promise the earliest results, slower acting but more fundamental and essential measures must also be taken. *These should aim at increasing productivity, efficiency and output throughout the economy, and at the restoration of a healthy, export-led rate of economic growth.* Augmenting the size of the labor force, inducing its restructuring by transfers from public and other services and from inefficient to more productive occupations and firms, and improving enterprise management and worker morale and productivity, are essential to the achievement of these goals. Day nurseries which would permit young mothers to join the labor force, lengthening the work week, deferring the retirement age, severe staff reductions in the bloated public services, the vesting of pension rights, protection of the seniority rights of workers who change to more productive jobs, the provision of rental housing for workers whose new job opportunities require a change of locale, the withdrawal of protection from inefficient firms, and the modification of working rules to permit management to achieve greater efficiency on the shop floor, would all contribute to the improvements necessary. Wage increases should be related to improved productivity, and a differential scale of tax or other incentives could be used to induce labor transfers to more productive and essential occupations. The assurance of income supports during the change-over period, and occupational re-training, where necessary, should support the necessary transfer process. To spur labor morale and productivity, control costs and help to control prices, we recommend that serious consideration be given by both employers and workers to the introduction of wage incentive, including profit-sharing, plans. All these measures would help to encourage needed investment, technology, greater competitiveness and exports. They would also help to improve the balance of payments.

In calling upon Israel to organize and carry through a truly national effort to subdue inflation and restore the nation's economic health, we are aware of the sacrifices this would impose on all groups within the nation. But we also believe that a demonstration by Israel that she is doing what only she can do to help herself will provide the best justification for the very substantial help she will still need from others. Despite an optimum effort on Israel's part, the combination of her enormous defense and debt service burdens would be too much for her to bear. Since it does not appear to be practicable to expect new levels of assistance from the United States to be increased substantially, it may be more practicable for Israel to seek the equivalent of more assistance by relief on the debt service side.

Broadly viewed, it is financially easier and politically more palatable for a donor to increase the amount of *net* aid to a recipient by liberalizing the terms of service on *past* debt than by increasing the gross volume of new aid extended. This can be done in a number of alternative or complementary ways. Part of the large existing debt could be converted retroactively into grants. Interest rates could be reduced. Existing periods of grace could be extended. Loan maturities could be re-scheduled. The grant-loan ratio on new assistance could be liberalized. Consideration of the enormous defense burden which Israel has borne and will need to continue to bear in the future — a large part of which the United States might otherwise have felt obliged, in the service of its own national interests, to incur — suggest to us that it would be reasonable for the United States Government to consider assisting Israel to regain her economic health by such means.

While practical opportunities for economic cooperation with Egypt may be larger than has been suggested by early studies, it is not clear how soon it will be practicable for these opportunities to be realized. Egypt as well as Israel must seek to implement the normalization of economic relations. Yet, Egypt too needs to improve economic conditions for its people, to demonstrate the fruitful results of the peace process, as well as to offset damaging external pressures and propaganda. Thus, while the progress and benefits of economic cooperation may not be swift, *development finance institutions capable of facilitating and financing such cooperation are nevertheless needed, and should be put in place in time to facilitate even the earliest stages of economic cooperation. It is in the interest of the U.S. and the West to fund such institutions and to extend to Israel and to Egypt the large scale assistance they will need to overcome their serious difficulties and to build and cement the peace.*

In the sturdier and more dynamic economic climate we envisage, Israel should be more attractive to foreign investors — non-Jewish as well as Jewish — than has been the case till now. This attraction should be greatest for firms best able to benefit from Israel's chief comparative economic advantages — an abundance of highly qualified scientific and technical manpower available at relatively low cost, backed up by first-rate research and development capabilities, and duty-free access to the U.S. and the Common Market for a wide variety of products. For those foreign investors whose organizational, financial, or personnel and time constraints are not conducive to establishing autonomous, branch or partnership operations in Israel, yet who desire a more direct investment association with Israel than that provided by the purchase of Government of Israel bonds, intermediate opportunities exist. The purchase of shares in Israeli investment institutions or, even more directly, foreign investor syndicates in partnership or association with Israeli investment banks and groups, provide opportunities which can be at once less demanding of personal involvement, more interesting and, of course, equally helpful to Israel's economic development, as well as financially rewarding.

Concerning Israel's social, religious and political problems, we can only urge that Israel recognize the urgent need for dealing with them. We shall however venture to make a specific comment on Israel's electoral *system*, only because it is clear that her basic problems can effectively be dealt with only by governments capable of making politically difficult decisions. The present proportional representation system which results in coalition rather than majority governments has not been able till now to produce governments with this capability. We therefore subscribe to the view expressed by many Israeli leaders in the past that this system, which has malfunctioned so persistently and with such grave consequences, should be reformed.

Israel's internal problems undoubtedly help to explain a significant though little-discussed and difficult to measure phenomenon — that of emigration from Israel (*Yerida*). The number of Israelis currently living abroad (*Yordim*), mostly in the U.S., is estimated to range from some 350,000 to 500,000 — at the higher level, approximately one for every six Jews living in Israel. What is novel about this phenomenon is that, in contrast to the emigration of earlier periods, when the emigrants were recent immigrants, we are dealing here with the emigration of established Israelis, many of them native-born. In the absence of adequate studies, the phenomenon is difficult to assess. We suspect however that its implications are profound, and that it bears importantly on the questions of Jewish identity, *aliyah* and the quality of life in Israel, as well as on relative opportunities in Israel and abroad. As of now, it is possible only to speculate as to why so many Israelis have left home, how many of them intend to and may actually return and how many others may follow them, possibly to live permanently abroad. It must be observed that this problem, like many others, is one which Israel does not seem to have addressed, much less resolved. Like many others, it requires early and serious attention. While we understand Israel's dismay, embarrassment and even resentment of the *yordim*, we permit ourselves two observations. First, it seems to us Israel must recognize that if, as a small economy with an extraordinarily high percentage of university graduates, she cannot offer suitable career opportunities to all of them at home, it is only to be expected that many of them will seek such opportunities abroad. Second, since so many have already left Israel and others undoubtedly will, a possible constructive response might be to accept these facts of life, and seek to devise programs involving the *yordim* which could be productive of positive benefits for Israel. Such programs could aim at personal financial contributions, remittances and savings and investment in Israel by Israeli expatriates. Expatriates might also serve as representatives for Israeli exporters, as staff for branch offices of Israeli firms and as volunteers in encouraging direct investments in Israel, in fund-raising, in teaching Hebrew, and in other communal activities.

Many, perhaps most, Israelis seem to hold quite parochial views about the Diaspora. They seem to have little interest in, or appreciation of, the ways of life, the communal interests, motivations, problems and sensitivities of the many and disparate Jewish communities of the

[117]

Diaspora. Even in the case of the better-known American Jewish community, there is inadequate appreciation of the diversity of views held, and of the increasing difficulties posed for Jewish leaders when they are expected unquestioningly to support Israel's policies regardless of the private reservations they may have about them. This lack of interest and appreciation has resulted, from time to time, in Government of Israel policies and actions which have seriously embarrassed national Jewish communities in one country or another. We recommend therefore that, in dealing with foreign governments, Israel show an active concern for the knowledge, sensitivities, concerns and interests of the Jewish communities in those countries, and consult with them, to the extent practicable.

As regards *aliyah*, the classic Zionist ideology which denigrates the prospects for a secure or meaningful Jewish existence in the Diaspora, and which conceives of Diaspora existence as living in exile, is remote from the thinking of most Jews who live in free democratic societies, and is not conducive to effective communications between Israelis and emancipated and secular Diaspora Jews. All Diaspora Jews have taken great pride in the creation, achievements and military prowess of Israel. The existence of the State, the fact of Jewish sovereignty and its ability to espouse not only its own cause but that of the entire Jewish people in international meetings, has afforded them great moral support. But despite this, the persistent hopes and efforts of Israeli leaders and Zionist organizations to achieve substantial increases in *aliyah* from Western Diaspora communities cannot confidently be counted upon to achieve far greater successes than they have in the past. Certain points concerning *aliyah* should therefore be made.

At any particular time, Jews inevitably immigrate to Israel, emigrate from Israel or change their minds about going to live in Israel. The balance of these movements is of great importance.

For Israelis, *aliyah*, especially voluntary *aliyah* from the West, represents reaffirmation of the Zionist postulate that Israel belongs to the entire Jewish people. Renewed *aliyah* signals to the Israelis that they are not alone, that other Jews are willing to share their burdens and are willing to accept physical insecurity, poorer social amenities and even a lower standard of living in return for the opportunity to live under Jewish sovereignty. Moreover, in view of *aliyah*, fewer young Israelis will consider leaving their country. *Aliyah* represents, for Israel, the addition of real resources. The skills, the enterprise, the work and civic habits of typical Western *olim* are urgently needed in Israel, where years of pressure of physical shortages and dependence on external resources have fostered centralization and reliance on slow and inefficient bureaucratic machines.

Obviously, a secure, prosperous and just Israel would be much more attractive to its own residents and to potential *olim* than a threatened, debt-ridden and strife-torn Israel. Recognition of this should impel the Israelis towards greater efforts to put their economic, social and political house in order. The rewards for successful efforts include not only improvement in domestic welfare but also chances for increased *aliyah* and decreased *yerida*.

In the final analysis, however, *aliyah* is a function of education in the broadest sense of the word. Since from an economic point of view Israel is unlikely to be able to compete with the most advanced Western countries for some time, other aspects must be stressed. These include spiritual values and acceptance of the premise that life under Jewish sovereignty is important and worthwhile. To achieve this objective it is necessary and desirable to expose Jewish youth as much as possible to life in Israel. To this end, more programs which entail spending time in Israel should be developed. These might include university study programs of the kinds already offered, as well as new programs to include more students, longer sessions, summer and winter tours, professional conferences, etc.

The effort, even if successful, is unlikely, considering past experience, to change radically the outlook and behavior of Jews in the Diaspora. Most will continue to stay in their homelands. Others may, with suitable encouragement, decide to spend part of their lives in Israel, establish a second home there, participate in an Israeli-based business, engage in volunteer work or take up a short term employment offer, such as a Sabbatical leave in an academic or research institution. Such activities merit further study and support.

Another important aspect is the educational experience of exposure to Israel and its problems which will be gained by all those involved, regardless of whether they stay in Israel or return to their countries of origin. In all likelihood, they will be more committed Jews with a deeper understanding of their people's problems and aspirations.

The question of *aliyah* extends also to Soviet Jewry, a question we have examined at some length in this Report. The issue has been posed in the following way: Should American Jewry continue to extend financial and other assistance to Soviet Jews who prefer to immigrate to the United States, or should the American Jewish community, by withholding such assistance, increase the relative attractions of Israel and thus help to lower the "dropout" rate among Jews leaving the Soviet Union? The chief arguments made for the withholding of such assistance have been:a) Israel needs them to ensure its security and future; b) Soviet Jewish emigres are not refugees; they have a national homeland waiting to welcome them; c) Israel cannot compete with the greater material inducements and opportunities offered by life in the U.S.,; d) Soviet Jews who emigrate to the U.S. and elsewhere in the West are likely soon to be assimilated; only in Israel can their continuity as Jews be assured; and e) The relatives these Soviet Jews leave behind in the Soviet Union are less likely to obtain permission to depart if those preceding them emigrate, not to Israel, but to some other country. On the other side of the issue, the chief argument has been a moral one: Soviet Jews, like all people, should be free to make their own choice of where they wish to live, and be assisted to do so. In our view, still other factors also need to be considered. The relative availability of jobs, housing and social services, the relative costs of absorption and the possible effects of expanded Soviet immigration in Israel on *yerida* all need to be weighed in the overall balance. Further, individual characteristics like age, health, work capabilities, the presence or absence of relatives and friends and personal readiness to adapt to a given new environment are also relevant. The question is indeed a difficult one. But since neither Israel nor the Diaspora organizations have been willing to take responsiblity for placing pressure on Soviet Jewish emigres to go to Israel against their wishes (the Jewish Agency could easily do this by withholding their referral to HIAS, which does not extend assistance without such referral), it would appear that Soviet Jewish emigres will continue to make a free choice as to where they wish to build their new lives.

The issue of Soviet Jewish emigres' destination came to the fore toward the end of the 1970's when an increasingly high dropout rate coincided with a liberalized Soviet emigration policy. This situation has now changed. A sudden reversal in Soviet policy reduced Jewish emigration sharply in 1980. By the third quarter of 1980 Soviet Jewish emigration was only 25% of the rate the year before. This sharp curtailment has added a new and weighty Jewish concern to that of the emigres' choice of ultimate destination.

To help meet Jewish needs in many Jewish communities throughout the world, and especially those of isolated Jewish communities, to develop a stronger sense of Jewish peoplehood, and to forge ever stronger ties between Israel and the Diaspora, we *recommend that Israel, with the active participation of the Diaspora, create a strong and dedicated Shalom Corps, whose members would spend a year or two abroad in response to requests from weaker communities for teachers, rabbis and other essential Jewish services.*

The Shalom Corps concept should also embrace the Diaspora. Young Jews in the Diaspora should be urged to volunteer for one or two years of service in Israel. Service could consist of work in border and agricultural settlements, social work, hospital work, teaching, urban renewal and other valuable communal programs.

It has also been suggested that an organization like the Shalom Corps should be assigned a major role in large scale national projects such as the Mediterranean-Dead Sea hydro-electric project, settlement building and important archeological "digs" and restorations.

In the past such projects have met with limited success because of the failure to provide the institutional frameworks needed to direct and administer part time volunteer contributions to such programs. Only the *kibbutzim* proved to have the flexibility needed, and indeed *kibbutzim* have attracted a large number of young people from around the world (many non-Jewish) who seek to spend several months in Israel. While the organization of volunteer work on a large scale is undoubtedly difficult, surely more institutions — the universities, hospitals, some government ministries and the Jewish Agency Youth and Hechalutz Departments — could be counted on to contribute their share in translating the idea of a Shalom Corps into reality.

Finally, because of our concern, our needs, and our hope that Israel will find ways progressively to embody in her way of life the values and goals which Judaism gave to the world, we venture to suggest — in the expectation that wiser heads will improve upon our thinking — four major paths towards this end which are appropriate to our times.

*First*, to strive for and progressively to move towards an ever greater degree of economic and social justice marked by social harmony, a quality of life nourishing to the spirit, and high ethical values. The kibbutz was a great social innovation in its day. A highly urbanized Israel is in need of others. The relations between oriental and occidental Jews, between Jewish and Arab Israelis, and problems of income distribution and housing are obvious priority areas for the application of social justice objectives.

*Second*, to build on and expand its earlier and current efforts and experience to be distinctively of service and benefit to the poor peoples of the world, by developing technologies appropriate to their needs and by technical assistance in the fields of agriculture, health, science and education. A technical arm of the above-mentioned Shalom Corps could also be significant in this connection, and provide opportunities for active participation to Diaspora Jews lacking in training for meeting Jewish needs in overseas communities.

*Third*, by continuing to contribute, creatively and outstandingly, to progress in science, ethics, religion, philosophy, the arts and all other endeavors which nourish and enrich civilization and all mankind.

*Fourth*, and perhaps most important, by seeking greater understanding of some of the basic dilemmas which confront modern man in the Western world: resource and pollution limitations on economic growth; the problem of man's relations to technology; the persistence of poverty amidst plenty; the alienation of urbanized man; the satisfaction of spiritual needs in an increasingly secular, materialistic world; the reconciliation of science and religion; and the perplexing relationship between liberty and equality — progress on such dilemmas as these would surely shine like a beacon throughout the world. Israel has, to be sure, many difficult internal and external problems to solve before her creative energies and gifts can be concentrated on such tasks. But ultimately who, better than Israel, with her heritage of Jewish values and philosophy, and her ability to involve the collaboration of creative Jews throughout the world, can more appropriately undertake to cope with such existential questions?

## On the Diaspora and Israel-Diaspora Relations

Most Diaspora Jews, wherever they may live, seem to have certain characteristics in common, albeit in varying degrees. In comparison with the majority of the people in the countries in which they live, they are on average better educated and enjoy higher than average incomes and occupational status. They are also of considerably higher than average age, and their lower than average birthrates point to the prospect of large future population declines. Despite individual differences and occasional sub-group countertrends, they are increasingly secular, intermarriage and assimilation continue to increase, and their children drift ever further from Judaism and Jewish communal concerns. These phenomena, it has been pointed out, have been repeated, historically, in or by the third generation of every emancipated Diaspora community.

With generational change, the problem of future Jewish leadership becomes increasingly acute. Combined with occupational shifts from business to the professions and academia, these trends presage a decline in communal fund-raising as well. Meanwhile, for most mature adults old enough to remember, the Holocaust, the creation of the State of Israel, and Israel's need for financial, moral and political support have rejuvenated their sense of Jewish identity, and meeting these needs has become for them the chief avenue for its expression.

Another noteworthy aspect of most Diaspora communities in the post-World War II era has been the striking changes in the size and/or composition of their Jewish populations, due to migratory movements. Apart from emigration to Israel, which virtually depleted some communities (e.g., that of Yemen), the most outstanding was the vast change in the Jewish community of Frace due to the immigration of North African Jewry. Even the U.S. Jewish community, the largest in the Diaspora, has been significantly altered in recent years by immigration from Israel, the Soviet Union, Iran and elsewhere.

Conclusions beyond these must distinguish among the different communities of the Diaspora. For convenience and brevity, we classify the Diaspora as comprised first, of Jews living lives of relative security in the free democratic societies of the Western world, and next, Jews living less secure, troubled, threatened, vulnerable or isolated lives in the Soviet Union and Communist bloc, in parts of Latin America and in other communities around the world.

## The Emancipated Communities

The security of Jews living in the free democratic societies of the West is only relative. Occasional demonstrations or acts of violence by extremist groups are reminders that anti-semitism is not dead, and that under certain conditions it might grow to serious proportions. But if the threats to their security *within* their national societies are dismissed by most as minor only, they do share with those societies the growing *external* insecurity which originates in Soviet expansionism, OPEC oil price aggression and supply control, Third World pressures and Middle East turmoil and instability. This perception however does not yet seem to be as widely held as it needs to be or as it may soon become.

The aging and population decline, intermarriage and assimilation, growing secularism and problems of generational change go hand in hand, at the same time, and especially in the highly-organized American Jewish community, with a plethora of organizations. Many of them are engaged in overlapping or duplicate activities which result in work lacking in depth and waste of available resources. *We recommend a serious joint study to eliminate unnecessary duplications and permit a strengthening of Jewish organizational activities through better allocated and more cooperative, coordinated and intensive efforts.*

With increasing visitations and contacts over the years, and the more intensive media coverage of Israel since President Sadat's visit in 1977, Diaspora Jews are better informed about conditions in Israel than formerly. Many see Israel more realistically, and are disturbed by what they see. They are disturbed by Israel's economic, social, religious and political problems, and by her inability to cope with them effectively. Many are also disturbed by Israel's policy stance in negotiations on the West Bank and Gaza Autonomy, and the indications that her settlements policies are not motivated solely or predominantly by security considerations. While these Diaspora Jews have always believed that only Israel was competent to decide on policies involving her security, they are now keenly aware of the sharp differences *within* Israel on these very questions — differences reflected within Israel's military establishment itself, as well as among officials responsible for the planning and implementation of settlements policies. Such differences within Israel have suggested to some Diaspora Jews that it was time for them also to end their self-imposed restraints and express their views on these questions.

The peace-making process however is only the latest and most delicate of the issues involved in the Israel-Diaspora relationship on which independently-minded Diaspora Jews, for the most part, have suppressed their differences and doubts. These extend over a wide range that includes Israel's internal economic and social problems, questions concerning specific Diaspora communities, and issues inherent in the Israel-Diaspora relationship itself.

That many Diaspora leaders, in their contacts with Israel, have stifled or understated their concerns, doubts and differences is not the fault of Israel. If many secular Diaspora Jews are heavily dependent on their concerns and support of Israel for their sense of Jewish identity, criticism and differences with Israel may have seemed to them to threaten to violate that bond and sense of identity, and hence presented them with an intolerable problem. In a more practical vein, another difficulty has also stood in the way. Within what existing or potential institutional or structural framework could representative views of the Diaspora be distilled and expressed? And how could the asymmetry between a sovereign state and such a representative Diaspora body be bridged or balanced so as to facilitate a full, free and constructive dialogue?

We believe the time has come for the Jewish leaders of the Diaspora to cast off the self-imposed restraints which have prevented them from candidly expressing their views and concerns in face-to-face discussions with Israeli leaders, especially where these concerns involved Israel and Israel-Diaspora relations. We believe that both Israel's and the Diaspora's best interests require this. *We therefore urge that when Israel and Diaspora representatives meet, they should put on the table and attempt to resolve the issues which have been festering in the absence of open discussion, to the end that a true partnership and consensus among the several components of the Jewish people may begin to be forged.*

This becomes all the more important as the Diaspora's financial contributions to Israel are reduced progressively to a smaller proportion of her external capital needs and, even more importantly, become less relevant to the solution of her manifold problems. New links with Israel therefore need to be forged to sustain the Jewish identity of secular Jews in the Diaspora.

Ideally, a body broadly representative of the diversity of the Diaspora should engage in constructive dialogue with the State of Israel on all issues and problems of mutual concern. The need for such a body has been recognized and advocated, in various ways, for many years. The inability of Soviet Jewry and a number of other Jewish communities to be represented in such a body does not strike us as a major obstacle. More important are the problems involved in seconding to the most representative international Jewish organization(s) those important Jewish national organizations not yet affiliated, in establishing that the Diaspora organization (or organizations) concerned truly represents and speaks for its (their) purported constituency, and in reaching a reasonable degree of consensus on key issues.

*We urge the World Jewish Congress, to which we submit this report, to take the lead in convoking the appropriate Jewish bodies and/or persons to consider and determine how this objective may best be achieved, and in carrying this project forward.* (See Supplementary Statement by Prof. Ben-Shahar.)

This report has been replete with suggestions and recommendations which require priority attention in the kind of Israel-Diaspora dialogue and forum we consider essential (see especially chapter five). We shall not recapitulate them here. We should like however, before closing, to address ourselves briefly to two questions previously unmentioned, and to one new proposal, all of which also warrant place on such an agenda.

On the matter of Jewish education, there is a strong body of opinion among both Israeli and Diaspora Jews that Jewish survival in the Diaspora depends on the development of a wide network of Jewish day schools in which all Jewish children could obtain a genuine and meaningful Jewish education. Equally strong views held by other, and perhaps most, Diaspora Jews maintain that Jewish children in democratic countries should be educated in public rather than parochial schools. A similar division appeared in the Commission's only discussion of the subject, and we made no attempt to reach a consensus on this important question. (See the Supplementary Statement by Avraham Agmon, Prof. Ben-Shahar and Naftali Blumenthal.)

We have noted in passing, but not pursued, the serious matter of the relative lack of involvement of Jewish intellectuals in the communal life of Diaspora Jewry. In a situation where voluntary organizational leadership is in the hands of busy men and women whose available time is preoccupied largely with operational matters, and whose professional staff are similarly heavily engaged, the time and perspective needed for forward planning and policy considerations are extremely limited. Certain institutions and organizations attempt to fill this void. We might name among them, although this does not pretend to be an exhaustive list, the Institute of Contemporary Jewry at the Hebrew University in Jerusalem, the Continuing (annual) Seminars held under the auspice of the President of Israel, several Institutes at the University of Tel Aviv, the Institute of Jewish Affairs (affiliated with the World Jewish Congress), the annual Israel-Diaspora dialogues organized by the American Jewish Congress, the Center for Jewish Community Studies, the National Jewish Resource Center, and the policy studies and papers developed by and under the auspice of the American Jewish Committee. We have not attempted to study how each of these (and others) contributes to the overall policy studies needs of world Jewry, or how their work might more effectively be coordinated better to serve those needs, or considered the question of whether there is need and room for a new policy studies institute which might play an overarching coordinating role and undertake to fill existing gaps in current study programs. We recommend that such a study be undertaken, and that it give special consideration to the need for what might be called an International Institute of Israel-Diaspora Affairs, to provide the policy analyses essential to the formulation of a cohesive strategy by Jewish decision-makers embracing the entire range of Israel-Diaspora relations. (On this point, see Prof. Ben-Shahar's Supplementary Statement.)

In assessing the nature and derivation of Israel's economic problems, we indicated that preoccupation at the top levels of government with other problems, excessive reliance on external resources and other factors had resulted in day-to-day crisis management of the country's economic affairs without regard to the longer term implications of *ad hoc* emergency decisions hastily made in a crisis atmosphere. To work her way constructively out of her present predicament, Israel needs a comprehensive, multi-year national economic plan.

*The time is overdue for a joint Israel-Diaspora effort to devise constructive solutions to Israel's basic economic problems.* It is hoped that the government of Israel and the major fundraising organizations and contributors will agree on this need. Such an effort would call for a comprehensive analysis of these problems; devise an overall plan and programs for dealing with them; assess the domestic and external resources required for executing the plan; explore the means for mobilizing the necessary resources; and, very importantly, outline in specific terms the economic policies — fiscal, monetary, investment, trade, manpower, energy, housing and so on — that would be necessary to facilitate implementation of the plan. Agreement on such a plan and its concomitant economic policies would not only spur the Diaspora communities to play their essential fund-raising and investment role to the full degree required — it would also strengthen their ability to enlist the support of their governments and major financial institutions for so major, essential and constructive an effort.

Ideally, the initiative for such an approach, at least in a formal sense, should come from the Government of Israel. The first operational step, after such an invitation, would be for the Diaspora organizations concerned to organize and send to Israel a group of truly outstanding financiers, industrialists, economists and engineers to work on the spot with a comparable non-partisan Israeli group designated by the government and major economic organizations like the Histadrut and the Manufacturers Association. It would be the task of the single economic commission jointly constituted by these groups to make the appropriate analyses and assessments, and to devise the corresponding plans, programs and policies. The teams would report their findings and recommendations to their respective principals within three months or so. After study on both sides, the principals would meet to arrive at a basic consensus, which could be kept up to date by a similar process for as long as was necessary or desirable.

A joint planning venture of this kind, we submit, has much to commend it. First, it appears to offer a promising way to ensure that

Israel's critical economic problems can systematically be addressed with reasonable hope of constructive solutions. Second, the non-politically aligned objectivity attached to Diaspora participation should help gain public acceptance of, or reduce political opposition in Israel to, a program jointly arrived at. Third, it would constitute a major step towards a new and real Israel-Diaspora working partnership. Fourth, by its very nature and prospective results, it would address and reduce, if not eliminate, a number of problems and issues which currently exacerbate the Israel-Diaspora relationship. Fifth, it would create an essential component for the long sought framework for a new Israel-Diaspora relationship. Finally, if successful, it could create conditions in Israel which would make it possible for the Jewish homeland to inspire and spiritually sustain Jewish life in the Diaspora.

We stated earlier that raising funds for Israel, and providing Israel with moral and political support in the native countries of the Diaspora communities, were becoming progressively less adequate either to living a satisfying Jewish life in the Diaspora, or to a satisfactory Israel-Diaspora relationship. We hope and trust however that if Israel moves along the lines we have stressed in this report as essential, and if the way is opened for the Diaspora to participate fully, in a continuing constructive dialogue, and with even more direct partnership involvement, in helping to shape a more secure and better future for Israel and the Jewish people, Jewish life in the Diaspora will take on a new and re-invigorated meaning, and the sense of Jewish identity will return to many in whom it has weakened almost to vanishing.

The problems we have outlined are grave indeed. Can Israel, in cooperation with the Diaspora and its friends, command the physical, organizational and moral resources needed to cope with them without disrupting the social fabric, endangering democracy or overstraining her economic capacity? A review of Israel's past suggests that her people have coped with more formidable challenges. Not only has Israel fought off successfully several attempts to annihilate her physically — with the help of the Jewish communities of the Diaspora and of friendly countries, she has managed to absorb hundreds of thousands of destitute, untrained immigrant refugees from Europe, North African, Iraq, Yemen and elsewhere within a very short span of time. Her people have settled a barren country, tamed the desert, established industries, and a modern infrastructure of facilities, institutions and social services.

Today's challenges, the challenges of peace, are not more awesome. They are however in a sense less immediate and, because they do not affect all groups in the same way or to the same degree, and because widely conflicting views prevail as to how they should be met, it is much more difficult to evoke a coherent, *united* response to them. What is needed is, first, a more realistic and general recognition and assessment of these new challenges, and second, the mobilization of the spirit and the determination to overcome them. These are the tasks that face Israel and world Jewry today. We must together resolve to undertake and see them through.

# Supplementary Statements

## By Avraham Agmon, Prof. Haim Ben-Shahar and Naftali Blumenthal

*We believe the Commission's statements on the important questions of Jewish education,* yordim *and* noshrim *are inadequate, and should be supplemented as stated below. Moshe Gitter, Ernest Japhet and Dan Tolkowsky have associated themselves with these views.*

### Jewish Education

Educational activities of common concern to Israel and the Diaspora should not be limited to those which relate to *aliya*. The concern with the need to counter the processes of assimilation and lack of identification with Judaism and with Israel which are becoming increasingly common among Jewish communities throughout the free world, and which pose a real danger to the future of the Jewish people is of vital importance. In the absence of large scale *aliya*, the only way to stem these processes, to maintain the centrality of Judaism and Israel, and to encourage the flowering of an authentic Jewish culture in keeping with our religious and national values is by encouraging Jewish education in the fullest sense. That is, the special elements of the Jewish spiritual and historical heritage should be acquired together with the full range of general subjects in a way which stimulates independent thought and individual growth. The combination of universalism with the value system rooted in the culture and civilization of the Jewish people throughout the millennia, in a comprehensive education process should show the relevance of the Jewish heritage to twentieth-century living.

The development and implementation of this concept of Jewish education presents a real challenge to Jewish educators in Israel and the Diaspora, for education cannot be divorced from the cultural environment in which the child lives. Great imagination and application is required to formulate programs, course material, and teaching methods that will permit each community to implement its educational program at all levels in keeping with local conditions.

It is proposed that the responsibility for designing and developing this approach and providing the supporting services necessary for its implementation be entrusted to a *World Jewish Education Center*. The Center would utilize the academic resources of Israeli and Diaspora institutions of higher learning, the experience gained in Israel's national system of Jewish education, the knowledge of Diaspora scholars, and the experience of Diaspora educators acquainted with local conditions. While allowing for a variety of educational philosophies, traditions and techniques in a single location, the Center will emphasize the common denominators of Jewish education and will provide all the benefits of intercommunity contacts without imposing a monolithic system. Because of the high concentration of Jewish scholars and educators in Israel, and because Israel has had the most experience of Jewish education that is total rather than supplementary, it would seem natural to locate the headquarters of the Center in Israel.

It must be emphasized that the Center should not attempt to impose any form of control on the institutions of Jewish education; rather it should constitute a source of inspiration and guidance for educators in Jewish communities all over the world.

Expanding the system of Jewish education along these lines will require substantial financial resources. It is proposed that part of the money raised by the Jewish appeals and currently allocated to Israel be used to finance the range of additional activities that would be generated by the concept underlying the World Jewish Education Center.

Although funding the expansion of the Jewish educational system in this way would entail a reduction in the flow of Appeals funds from the Diaspora to Israel, this will harm Israel's economy only marginally. Much of this budget would still be transferred to Israel — no longer as aid, but as payment for educational services. Using these funds to pay Israel for services to world Jewish education will ultimately prove more beneficial both to Israel and to the Jewish people in the Diaspora, and will also liberate both Israel and the Diaspora from the negative psychological effects of a one-sided relationship of dependence.

## Yordim and Noshrim

Having discussed *aliyah* in the context of Jewish migration, we should also briefly consider the questions of *yerida* — the emigration of Israelis, including young people born in Israel — and *neshira* — the migration of Soviet emigrants to countries other than Israel. The existence of these phenomena is, as was noted above, distressing and even embarrassing to Israeli and Diaspora leaders alike. They represent, especially in the case of *yerida*, a failure in the educational process; they are indicative of grave shortcomings in Israel's polity, society and economy. Those who leave indicate their unwillingness to continue carrying the burden associated with living under Jewish sovereignty. The reasons can be many — economic, social, political, personal; possibly a combination of all factors. The result is the same — Israel is weakened and those who are left behind have a heavier burden to carry.

*Neshira* is perhaps easier to understand, bearing in mind that those concerned have few Jewish roots and no Zionist traditions. In their case, the wish to leave Soviet Russia is the major motive for their request to come to Israel. Once they leave, many choose what seem to them greener pastures. In this case, too, many Israelis are disappointed to note that so few Jews who were persecuted because of their Jewishness choose to share the Israelis' life, aspirations, achievements and burdens.

How should *noshrim* and *yordim* be treated by Jewish organizations in the U.S. and Europe? It is not easy to answer that question, but failure to formulate an answer is in this case also an answer. The question should therefore be addressed. We subscribe wholeheartedly to the idea that every person has a basic inalienable right to leave his country if he so chooses. It is on the basis of this premise that the world has supported the demand of the Russian Jews to emigrate. This right belongs also to every Israeli. On the other hand, we see no reason why Jewish organizations should help other Jews to settle outside Israel where they are free to come and go as they please, just because they do not want to live there.

The arguments against this view are compelling and cannot be lightly dismissed. If *yordim* and *noshrim* are not helped, and in one way or another encouraged to integrate into the Jewish community in the Diaspora, they may choose assimilation, an outcome which is worse from a Jewish point of view. Not less compelling is the argument that if *noshrim* and *yordim* are "sinners" in some sense then failure to live in Israel is also a "sin" which *yordim* and *noshrim* share with the rest of the Diaspora community. Why, in other words, should Diaspora Jews who have elected to stay in the Diaspora persecute or punish other Jews who want to share their life? These arguments are countered by the view that if official Jewish assistance is given to *noshrim* and, much worse, to *yordim*, *yerida* and *neshira* will increase even further. We find this argument compelling and overriding, and therefore side with those who oppose aid to *yordim* and *noshrim*.

## On Peace

Mssrs. Agmon, Ben-Shahar and Blumenthal also recommended the deletion of parts of paragraphs 1 and 2 in the Summary Conclusions and Recommendations, because they believe we should refrain from commenting on the tactics of either Israel or Egypt in the peace process.

## Prof. Haim Ben-Shahar

# Jewish Policy Studies

This report suggests that peace, whether partial or comprehensive, clearly ushers in a new era into Jewish life. The Jewish agenda gets crowded with new issues requiring fresh analysis and possibly new answers. The pragmatic answers provided by ad hoc decisions by Israel's government, the Jewish Agency and a host of other organizations do not necessarily amount to a cohesive strategy capable of dealing with these issues. Decisions must be made by the competent leadership both in Israel and the Diaspora. They could, however, be much improved if they were based on systematic analysis of the questions confronting us, including identification of the problems, assessment of responses and ways of implementing them.

The activity of this Commission illustrates the way in which these needs could be met. Its investigations and deliberations have highlighted the importance of an independent framework for greater cooperation between leaders and scholars, decision makers and researchers, Israel and the Diaspora. In order to ensure that the problems of both Israel and the Diaspora will continue to receive the thorough attention they require, it is recommended to establish an *International Institute of Israel-Diaspora Affairs* using world Jewry's finest resources — intellectual figures and community leaders experienced in the formulation and implementation of political strategies. Operating simultaneously in Israel and in main Diaspora centers, this independent Institute would establish study groups and working commissions to identify central problems, conduct research, and propose well thought-out and innovative policies and programs of action. It will then bring these programs to the attention of the relevant institutions in Israel and the Diaspora, and encourage them to take appropriate steps to promote their implementation.

# On Israel-Diaspora Relations

Prof. Ben-Shahar felt strongly that the recommendation made in Para. 35, Summary Conclusions and Recommendations, should open with the following formulation: "Ideally, a representative body reasonably competent to speak for Israel as well as the entire Diaspora should engage in constructive discussion on all issues and problems of mutual concern. The need for such a body has been recognized for many years. It would permit all concerned to express ideas and reservations in an atmosphere of cooperation rather than conflict, which would enhance the sense of partnership and common destiny."

# Personal Statement by Mrs. Liliane Winn

"I hope that the work of this Commission will be the initiating factor for Israel having a model social order, self-sustained by a strong economy, fueled by export of native technology; a vehicle for *real* Israel-Diaspora relations; a Jewish renaissance — providing resources for free Jewish day schools world-wide; Jews of Sephardi origin to enter the mainstream of Jewish life thereby enriching the heritage of all Jews."

# List of Papers and Presentations

(P) Presented to Meetings of the Commission and
(D) Distributed to the Commission

## BASIC WORKING PAPERS

1. (D) Walinsky, Louis J., "Working Paper #1 (design for the Commission's study)
2. (P) Walinsky, Louis J., "Summary Preview of the Final Report" (presented to International Economic and Social Commission meeting of January 28-29, 1980)

## PEACE PROCESS

3. (P) Agmon, Avraham, "World Jewry and the Peace Building Process: Jewish Economic Concerns" (presented to International Economic and Social Commission meeting September 4, 1979)
4. (D) Avineri, Shlomo, "Political Relations", *If Peace Comes* (Van Leer Jerusalem Foundation, 1978)
5. (D) Eban, Abba, "Israel: Between Conflict and Peace", *Worldwide January/February 1979* (based on presentation to World Jewish Congress Symposium, November 3, 1978)
6. (D) Gafny, Arnon, "The Economic and Social Basis for a Stable Peace" (presentation at Symposium 'The Substance of Peace', sponsored by the Center for Information & Documentation on Israel, The Hague, Holland, June 13, 1979)
7. (D) Hirsch, Seev, "How Can The Jewish Community Help With the Peace Process?", February 12, 1979
8. (D) Hirsch, Seev, "The Middle East Development Corporation", September 24, 1979
9. (D) Kissinger, Henry A., "The Challenges of Peace", *Worldview January/February 1979* (based on presentation to World Jewish Congress Symposium, November 3, 1978)

---

***Included in Summary of Meeting

10. (P) Rabinovitch, Itamar, "Possible Peace Scenarios" (presented to International Economic and Social Commission meeting March 14, 1979)

## ISRAEL

11 (D) A.I.D., "Report on the Israeli Economy and Debt Repayment Prospects" (as submitted to the Committee on Foreign Relations, United States Senate, January 15, 1980)

12. (P) Ben-Shahar, Haim, "Restructuring Israel's Economy" (presented to International Economic and Social Commission meeting September 3, 1979)

13. (P) Berglas, Eitan, "Short Term Perspectives" (presented to International Economic and Social Commission meeting September 3, 1979)

*** (P) Blumenthal, Naftali, (Presentation to International Economic and Social Commission meeting September 5, 1979)

14. (D) Center for Jewish Community Studies Staff Report, "Project Renewal: An Introduction to the Issues and Actors", January 1980

15. (D) Crittenden, Ann, "Israel's Troubled Economy", *Moment, November 1979* (reprinted from Foreign Affairs, Summer 1979)

16. (P) Eisenstadt, Shmuel, "Israel Society in Transition from War to Peace" (presented to International Economic and Social Commission meeting September 4, 1979)

17. (D) Feige, Edgar L., "The Economic Consequences of Peace in the Middle East", *Challenge, January/February 1979*

18. (D) Gitelman, Zvi, "The Other Dimension: Crisis and Cleavage in Israel" (background for Discussion, Board of Governors Institute February 9-12, 1978, American Jewish Committee)

19. (D) Gitelson, Susan Aurelia, "Israel and The Third World", *Judaism, Spring 1980*

20. (D) Goldmann, Nahum, "Zionist Ideology and The Reality of Israel", *Foreign Affairs*

21. (D) Hareven, Alouph, "The Right to Re-interpret: The Jewish Identity of Israel in the Future", *Lecture at Bar Ilan University on March 8, 1979* (Van Leer Jerusalem Foundation)

22. (P) Hirsch, Seev, "Short Term Economic Implications of Peace for Israel: Economic Relations with Egypt" (presented to International Economic and Social Commission meeting March 15, 1979)

---

***Included in Summary of Meeting

\*\*\*   (P)   Japhet, Ernest I., (Presentation to International Economic and Social Commission meeting September 5, 1979)

23.   (D)   Jerusalem Post, "Setting the record straight on emigration", March 24, 1980

\*\*\*   (P)   Kollek, Teddy, "The Role of Jerusalem" (presented to International Economic and Social Commission meeting September 5, 1979)

24.   (D)   Levinson, Jacob, "Reducing the Inflationary Vortex", *The Jerusalem Post, January 16, 1979*

25.   (D)   Levinson, Jacob, *"The Israel-Egypt Peace Treaty: Prospects for Economic Cooperation"* (Bank Hapoalim B.M., January 1979)

26.   (P)   Levinson, Jacob, "Three Way Ventures in the Middle East" (presented to International Economic and Social Commission meeting September 4, 1980

27.   (D)   Ministry of Finance, Israel, "Capital Imports to Israel by Source 1949-1977" (table)

28.   (P)   Razin, Assaf, "Israel's Economy after the Redeployment Period" (presented to International Economic and Social Commission meeting September 3, 1979)

\*\*\*   (P)   Shapira, Jonathan, "Comments on Prof. Zvi Gitelman's paper 'The Other Dimension: Crisis and Cleavage in Israel'" (Presentation to International Economic and Social Commission meeting September 3, 1979)

29.   (P)   Shimshoni, Daniel, "The Agenda for Social Policy" (presented to International Economic and Social Commission meeting September 4, 1979)

30.   (P)   Walinsky, Louis J., "Some Short Term Economic Consequences of the Peace" (presented to International Economic and Social Commission meeting March 14, 1979)

31.   (D)   Walinsky, Louis J., "Israel: Some Origins of the Current Malaise", August, 1979

## DIASPORA

32.   (D)   Bachi, Roberto, "The Demographic Crisis of Diaspora Jewry" (Background paper #4 prepared for the President of Israel's continuing seminar on World Jewry and the State of Israel, 1979)

33.   (D)   Hertzberg, Arthur, "Diaspora Dissent", *The Nation, March 22, 1980*

\*\*\*   (P)   Hirsch, Seev, "Comments on Prof. Bachi's paper 'The Demographic Crisis of Diaspora Jewry'" (Presentation to International Economic and Social Commission meeting April 29, 1980)

---

\*\*\*Included in Summary of Meeting

34. (D) Institute of Jewish Affairs/World Jewish Congress, "*Jewish Communities of the World*", Third Revised Edition 1971 (Crown Publishers Inc. 1972)

35. (D) Institute of Jewish Affairs, "*Proceedings of the Experts Conference on Latin America and The Future of its Jewish Communities, New York, June 3–4, 1972*"

*** (P) Jacobson, Charlotte, "Soviet Jewry: Problems and Issues" (presented to International Economic and Social Commission meeting April 29, 1980)

36. (P) Jacobson, Gaynor I., "Implications of Peace for Jewish Migration" (presented to International Economic and Social Commission meeting March 14, 1979)

37. (D) Kass, Drora and Lipset, Seymour M., "Israelis in Exile", *Commentary Magazine, November 1979*

38. (D) Kass, Drora and Lipset, Seymour M., "Contemporary Jewish Immigration to America: Israelis and Others", January 1980

39. (P) Klutznick, Philip M., "Present Condition of World Jewry: An Overview" (presented to International Economic and Social Commission meeting March 14, 1979)

*** (P) Kovadloff, Jacob, "Latin America Jewry" (Presented to International Economic and Social Commission meeting April 29, 1980)

40. (D) Mann, Theodore R., "Peace in the Middle East — The Role of the American Jewish Community" (Presentation to Plenary Session, National Jewish Community Relations Advisory Council, January 21, 1979)

41. (D) Ritterband, Paul and Cohen, Steven M., "Will the Well Run Dry? The Future of Jewish Giving in America", *Policy Studies 1979* (National Jewish Conference Center)

*** (P) Rothschild, Guy de, "Comments on French Jewry" (presented to International Economic and Social Commission meeting April 29, 1980)

42. (D) Samuelson, Arthur, "Argentine Jewry" (prepared for International Economic and Social Commission, August 1979)

43. (D) Samuelson, Arthur, "French Jewry" (prepared for International Economic and Social Commission, August 1979)

44. (D) Samuelson, Arthur, "Rumanian Jewry" (prepared for International Economic and Social Commission, August 1979)

45. (D) Shapiro, Leon, "Soviet Jewry Since the Death of Stalin: A 25-Year Perspective", Preprinted from *American Jewish Year Book, Vol. 79, 1979* (The American Jewish Committee, Institute of Human Relations, December 1978)

\*\*\* (P) Singer, Israel, "The American Jewish Community" (presented to International Economic and Social Commission meeting April 29, 1980)

46. (D) "World Jewish Population" (tables), *American Jewish Year Book, 1979, 1980*

## ISRAEL-DIASPORA RELATIONS

47. (D) Abramov, S.Z., "On Whose Behalf Did He Speak?", *Haaretz Commentary, 1979*

48. (D) American Jewish Committee International Task Force Report, *"Israel and American Jewish Interaction"*, 1978

49. (D) Aron, Raymond, "Selected Comments on Israel-Diaspora Relations", January, 1980

50. (D) Ben-Shahar, Haim, "Israel and the Diaspora — The Coming Decade", December, 1979

51. (D) Ben-Shahar, Haim, "Questions for Consideration on Issues in Israel-Diaspora Relations", Memo of July 9, 1979

52. (D) Bronfman, Edgar M., "Needed: A Really New Dialogue", *World Jewish Congress News and Views, February-March 1980*

53. (P) Bronfman, Edgar, M., "A New Instrument for a New Dialogue" (presented to International Economic and Social Commission meeting April 30, 1980)

54. (D) Chernin, Albert D., "A Survey of World Jewry and the Role and Responsibility of the American Jewish Community", *Journal of Jewish Communal Service, Winter, 1978, Vol. LV-No. 2*

55. (D) Dulzin, Arye L., Address to General Assembly, Council of Jewish Federations, Montreal, November 1979

56. (D) Ginzberg, Eli, "Israel and American Jews: The Economic Connection" (prepared for the Task Force on American Jewish-Israel Community Relationship, Jerusalem, January 1977)

57. (D) Goldmann, Nahum, "Reflections on the Israel-Diaspora Relationship" (prepared for International Economic and Social Commission meeting April 29-30, 1980)

58. (D) Goldmann, Robert B., "Some American Jewish Perspectives on the Relationship Between Israel and the American Jewish Community" (based on interviews with American Jewish leaders for Task Force meeting American Jewish Committee 1976)

59. (D) Hertzberg, Arthur, "Some Reflections on Zionism Today", *Being Jewish in America: The Modern Experience* (Schocken Books, 1978)

---

\*\*\*Included in Summary of Meeting

60. (P) Hertzberg, Arthur, "Reflections on Israel-Diaspora Relations" (presented to International Economic and Social Commission meeting April 30, 1980)

61. (P) Hoffberger, Jerold C., "Reflections on Israel-Diaspora Relations" (presented to International Economic and Social Commission meeting April 30, 1980)

62. (D) Jakobovits, Immanuel, "A Rabbi's Duty to Face Reality", *Jerusalem Post International Edition, February 24-March 1, 1980*

63. (D) Lerner, Natan, "Israel-Diaspora Relations: The Institutional Framework" (prepared for International Economic and Social Commission)

64. (P) Liebman, Charles S., "Implications of Peace for Israel-Diaspora Relations" (presented to International Economic and Social Commission meeting March 14, 1979)

65. (D) Liebman, Charles S., "Political Relationships Between Israel and American Jewry"

66. (P) Lipset, Seymour M., "Some Implications of Middle East Peace for Relations Between Israel and the Diaspora" (presented to International Economic and Social Commission meeting March 14, 1979)

67. (D) Samuelson, Arthur H., "Israel and the Diaspora: A Review of the Current Discussion" (prepared for International Economic and Social Commission)

\*\*\* (P) Symposium, "World Jewry and the Peace Process", Henry Kaufman, Philip M. Klutznick and Robert R. Nathan (presentations to International Economic and Social Commission meeting September 4, 1979)

68. (D) Vital, David, "Israel and Jewry: Digging In", *Midstream, November 1976)*

69. (D) Vital, David, "Dissenting Statement", *Israel and American Jewish Interaction* (American Jewish Committee Task Force Report, July 1978)

70. (P) Walinsky, Louis J., "Towards Economic Partnership in the Israel-Diaspora Relationship" (presented to International Economic and Social Commission meeting April 30, 1980)

71. (D) Yehoshua, A.B., "The Golah — As a Neurotic Solution", *Forum 35*

## MISCELLANEOUS

72. (D) Kraft, Joseph, "Letter from Egypt", *The New Yorker, May 28, 1979*

73. (D) Walinsky, Louis J., "Arab Investments and Influence in the United States" (prepared for American Jewish Committee, October 1978)

# A Commentary on the Report

## by Abba Eban

There are forceful passages in the World Jewish Congress report, and I certainly accept the assumption that it was written by people who care about Israel and seek its welfare. There are passages that are marked by a healthy realism concerning the eroding image of Israel in world opinion and the fact that Israel is not being replenished by aliyah and is being depleted by *yeridah*. This realism, however, becomes exaggerated when instead of describing a process, the authors describe the conditions they do as permanent. I have no objection to the statement that, historically, Jews have always been divided between the impulse to ingather, to close in on themselves, to live within their own terms, their own tongue, faith, land, patrimony, their own particularity, the impulse that led to Israel's rebirth, and, on the other hand, the impulse to pour their energies into all the oceans of universal history, to seek interaction with other cultures, the impulse to disperse. These two impulses have always worked together. An ideology that pretends that there is only a single direction in which Jewish history moves cannot be vindicated either by scholarship or by reality.

I am very uncomfortable with an ideology that has no relationship to reality and therefore loses touch with reality. Whether or not I negate the Diaspora, it continues, as a reality, to exist. So if I do negate it, all that I accomplish is the psychological result of my negation. You cannot build harmony or cooperation on the basis of such negation and the antagonism it provokes.

So far, so good. But the report goes far beyond that. It *consecrates* the present division between the Diaspora and Israel. It does not pay adequate tribute to the centrality of Israel to Jewish survival. And, above everything else, it has a rather tutelary, patronizing tone.

And it sells Israel short. To give just one example, it simply fails in truth. In order to make a case for changing the electoral system—which I would like to see changed—it makes the preposterous statement that Israeli governments have never been able to take politically daring decisions. Now that is absolutely ridiculous. No country in the world has ever been such a factory for the mass production of politically difficult decisions: the decision to establish the State; the decision to accept the armistice agreements; the decision to accept German reparations; the decision to go into Sinai in '56; the decision to withdraw from Sinai in '57; the decision not to fight immediately in '67; the decision to fight; the decision to cease fire; the decision to give up the whole of Sinai for a peace treaty. In other words, it's simply ridiculous to say that Israel has been inhibited in its power of decision by the election system. We have not always made the right decision, but we have never shied away from making difficult decisions, right or wrong. And the result of the report's perspective on this is to inflate the importance of the electoral system beyond any sensible proportion.

When a group like this suggests that Israeli politics is "demeaning," it is very hard for Israelis to take what it says seriously. The report was, after all, written in America a few years after Watergate and Vietnam. I find it absurd to say that Israel has not taken politically daring decisions. And that is just one example of the disconcerting externality of the report.

The report alleges that "There is a general sense that the Jewish goals and values Zionists hoped would flourish in the Jewish State are in an advanced state of erosion and are in danger of being permanently lost." This is a dangerous view. It is one thing to take a critical look at our society, but it is not very helpful to compare our society with an impossibly utopian image that could not possibly be sustained in historic terms. And one looks, after all the criticism, for some affirmation of faith, some sound of the trumpet, or for some less contemptuous evaluation of Israel's place in the world. There's too much about "this little, poor, young country." Well, we're not all that little; there are 60 countries with populations smaller than ours. We're not all that poor; there are about 100 of the 153 countries, in fact, about 110, with per capita incomes lower than ours. We're not all that young; we were the fifty-ninth member of the United Nations where there are now 153. So, we're one of the oldest countries in terms of modern sovereignty. And we're not all that backward a country: of the 153, there are about 130 that would envy Israel its scientific and technological infrastructure. After all the criticism, one misses an acknowledgement of Israel's extraordinary takeoff within a single generation to the forefront of progressive freedom and democracy and productivity. With a population of three and a quarter million, our export earnings go over the 10 billion dollar mark. This may be the highest per capita rate in the world.

Above everything else, the relationship between the Diaspora and Israel is stated not inaccurately, but much too statically. The report doesn't ask the question, "Must this always be the case, ought it not to change?" And then when the President of the World Jewish Congress speaks, *ex cathedra*, he says not only, "Is this the situation?" but also, "This is the way it's going to be; our children and our grandchildren are not going to have anything to do with coming to Israel." I'm not sure how anybody knows that. There's that television spot that you used to have here—perhaps you still have it—"It's 11 p.m.; do you know where your children are?" If that's the case, why not ask if you know where your grandchildren will be 20 years from now? I'm not sure that the grandchildren of present American Jewish leaders might not, in some cases, find their way to Israel. So there's a lack of dynamism about the report.

On the Israel side, with all due respect to the Israeli members of the Commission, they didn't really probe Israeli opinion. The Israeli members included six bankers and one economist. Now, if there was to be a discussion on inflation, I doubt they would have taken six people who had written books on Jewish history. Bankers have a professional commitment to the present reality; they're very skeptical about such things as the future, about things that are contingent. I therefore think that something went wrong with the operation in selecting the writer and in selecting the panel and in the final balance of the conclusion. So, although there is a good deal of useful material, most Israelis find something discordant about the report—more in its tone, perhaps, than in its content.

The report asks to what extent Israel is good for the Diaspora, and not to what extent are Israel and the Diaspora together good for the Jewish condition, for Jewish destiny. This is surely an example of a Diaspora-oriented approach, proceeding from the conviction that the function of Israel in the world is to provide the otherwise rudderless Jews of the Diaspora with a sense of vicarious location.

Are we in Israel giving you enough pride? Are we giving you enough sense of spiritual fulfillment? The report doesn't specifically raise the question of whether Diaspora Jewry is giving Israel that of which Diaspora Jewry is capable. It doesn't ask if the contribution of Jews to Israel's economy is commensurate with Diaspora capacities. Is there anything to be learned from the fact that Israel receives from the Diaspora less than ten percent of what it needs in terms of foreign currency support, or from the fact that Israel's export earnings are ten times as great as the combined revenues of all Jewish appeals, bond drives and university funds put together. Shouldn't American and Diaspora Jewry be doing more to correct the absence of aliyah? Are there not some ideological inhibitions that need to be addressed? All this reflects a serious imbalance in perspective.

The World Jewish Congress can play a useful role. That doesn't mean that if the WJC didn't exist we'd be sitting around wondering how to create it. It has its roots in organizational history, even in personal history and biography. But since it does exist we should make the best use of it, and see to it that it applies its energies in the most fruitful way. The prospect of a serious dialogue on Israel-Diaspora relations is very healthy. And the WJC has already fulfilled a very useful function in the international field, especially in areas where Israel cannot operate with complete freedom. I very much hope that in this area, as in others, it will, under its new president, embark on new initiatives.

I am especially concerned with the matter of Israel-Diaspora relations, which are today in an authentic condition of crisis. If the WJC can play a helpful role here, that would be very important. Over the past four years, the distance between Israel and the Diaspora has grown. I have the feeling that for the first time, the leaders of the Israeli government have not been the universally recognized spokesmen for the universal Jewish cause. The present government did not manage to establish the kind of rapport with the Diaspora that its predecessors had. The governments in which I served—especially Golda, Sapir and I—were in an intimate union of spirit with Diaspora Jews. And that has not been the case with our successors.

Moreover, there is an element of crisis that arises from concern regarding the Jewish character of Israel, which is related, in turn, to the failure of Diaspora Jewry to replenish Israel through aliyah. That is the central failure of Zionism. And that is why I think that after our elections, whatever the government that emerges, it would be well advised to hold a very solemn and far-reaching consultation with Diaspora Jews, perhaps in the form of a Congress that would be as memorable as the First Zionist Congress. We must learn how to discuss our common Jewish future; we must have an operative discussion about what the Jews in Israel and the Jews in the Diaspora can do to give a new thrust to our common struggle for survival and progress.

*Reprinted with permission from* Moment *magazine (May 1981, Vol. 6 No. 5)*